Astra and Sebastian
An Epic Love Story

L. W. Illsley

ASTRA AND SEBASTIAN is an epic adventure in the tradition of an ancient hero myth, but brought up to date by having two heroes, a man *and* a woman, thus presenting the story from both perspectives and also showing how perceived earthly opposites are reconciled by the universe.

Astra and Sebastian deals specifically with the change from child to adult but – as with any hero myth – this journey is applicable to any transitional moment in life. Hero myths throughout history articulate the symbolic journey of self discovery or individuation using archetypal motifs that we find in the unconscious. Cultures would build this psychological profile into their stories to aid the physical journey through life. Even today in a secular society, without help from any formal mythology, we undertake the journey of a hero unconsciously, every time we fall in love, face a crisis, or change, and any time we embark on a project.

L. W. ILLSLEY, originally from Trewellard on the west cliffs of Cornwall, now lives in East London where he writes and performs music as well as writing poetry. An avid reader since a boy, it was through music that he first discovered writing. He began, aged sixteen, by writing lyrics on receipt rolls when he worked on a supermarket checkout in Cornwall. Seven years later, and in a London supermarket, he wrote the two thousand line draft of his first epic poem also on receipt rolls. His entry to the Proverse Prize is his second completed epic poem.

Proverse Prize Finalist 2010

Astra and Sebastian
An Epic Love Story

Proverse Prize Finalist 2010

L. W. Illsley

Illustrated by Shelley Knowles-Dixon

Proverse Hong Kong

Astra and Sebastian

Astra and Sebastian: An Epic Love Story
by L. W. Illsley.
1st published in Hong Kong by Proverse Hong Kong, 22 November 2011.
Copyright © Proverse Hong Kong, 22 November 2011.
ISBN 978-988-19932-4-3

Distribution (Hong Kong and worldwide): The Chinese University Press of Hong Kong, The Chinese University of Hong Kong, Shatin, New Territories, Hong Kong SAR.
E-mail: cup-bus@cuhk.edu.hk Web site: www.chineseupress.com
Tel: [INT+852] 3943-9800; Fax: [INT+852] 2603-7355
Distribution (United Kingdom): Enquiries and orders to Christine Penney, Stratford-upon-Avon, Warwickshire CV37 6DN, England.
Email: <chrisp@proversepublishing.com>
Enquiries: Proverse Hong Kong, P. O. Box 259, Tung Chung Post Office, Tung Chung, Lantau Island, NT, Hong Kong, SAR China.
E-mail: proverse@netvigator.com Web site: www.proversepublishing.com
The right of L. W. Illsley to be identified as the author of this work has been asserted by him in accordance with the Copyright, Designs and Patents Act 1988.

Printed in Hong Kong by Artist Hong Kong Company, Unit D3, G/F, Phase 3, Kwun Tong Industrial Centre, 448-458 Kwun Tong Road, Kowloon, Hong Kong.
All original illustrations, including cover image, by Shelley Knowles-Dixon.
Permission from Shelley Knowles-Dixon to use these illustrations is warmly acknowledged.
Page design by Proverse Hong Kong. Cover design, Shelley Knowles-Dixon / Artist Hong Kong Company.

All rights reserved. No part of this publication may be reproduced, stored in a retrieval system, or transmitted, in any form or by any means, electronic, mechanical, photocopying, recording or otherwise, without the prior written permission of the publisher or publisher and author. The book is sold subject to the condition that it shall not, by way of trade or otherwise, be lent, re-sold, hired out or otherwise circulated without the publisher's – or author's and publisher's – prior written consent in any form of binding or cover other than that in which it is published and without a similar condition including this condition being imposed on the subsequent owner or purchaser. Please contact Proverse Hong Kong in writing, to request any and all permissions (including but not restricted to republishing, inclusion in anthologies, translation, reading, performance and use as set pieces in examinations and festivals).

Proverse Hong Kong

    British Library Cataloguing in Publication Data

Illsley, L. W.
  Astra and Sebastian : an epic love story.
  1. Epic poetry, English.
  I. Title II. Knowles-Dixon, Shelley.
  821.9'2-dc22

ISBN-13: 9789881993243

Astra and Sebastian

My thanks reaches out to my darling Shelley; to my ever supportive friends, Tom, Stu, Ben and Steph; to my family, Judith and Rachael Illsley and to Moira Knowles and Ivan Dixon; thanks also for the insightful proof-reading by Steph Haxton and to all those who've listened, supported and influenced me on this fantastic journey, in particular Gillian Bickley and the team at Proverse Hong Kong. I am forever grateful.

And also to Joseph Campbell. For without his fantastic work, "The Hero With A Thousand Faces", none of this would have been possible.

Astra and Sebastian

"The truths contained in religious doctrines are after all so distorted and systematically disguised that the mass of humanity cannot recognize them as truth. The case is similar to what happens when we tell a child that newborn babies are brought by the stork. Here, too, we are telling the truth in symbolic clothing, for we know what the large bird signifies. But the child does not know it. They hear only the distorted part of what we say, and feel that they have been deceived; and we know how often their distrust of the grown-ups and their refractoriness actually take their start from this impression. We have become convinced that it is better to avoid such symbolic disguisings of the truth..."
—Sigmund Freud

"It has always been the prime function of mythology and rite to supply the symbols that carry the human spirit forward."
—Joseph Campbell

"Truth is one, the sages speak of it by many names."
— The Vedas

Astra and Sebastian

Contents

1.   The Cave   17
We meet our heroine Astra, an orphan, meditating in a cave on a lonely mountain. The story begins as she realises the time has come for her to return to the mêlée of the town, far away in a valley, a town dominated by a castle upon a hill. It is a place she left many years ago having never quite fitted in.

2.   Meanwhile In The Market   19
Sebastian is introduced pushing the family cart to market with his father Sebastian the elder. Once inside the castle, where the market is held, Sebastian goes off to help his mother, Julia, carry water for the merchants and customers.

3.   Home   22
The day has reached its end and Sebastian is taken home by Julia where they prepare the evening meal and tell stories until Sebastian the elder arrives. Their light-heartedness ceases and they become serious as he takes charge.

4.   A Day Of Knights   25
Sebastian awakes to a procession of knights from the castle and is enthralled. But his father warns him of the dangers behind the glamour.

5.   Which Witch Is Which   28
Although his father is not convinced, Sebastian is sent by his mother for lessons in healing and philosophy from an old woman who lives in the forest. The old woman is thought by the people who work in and around the castle to be a witch. She gives him a gift of wax to help him with his journey.

6.   Keep The Home Fires Burning   30
At the end of the day Sebastian returns from his lesson to the shocking discovery that his town is on fire. The black knights from the next town have set it alight in retribution for an attack

Astra and Sebastian

on them; an attack that began with the procession Sebastian had been so impressed with that very morning. He runs home, only in time to see his father being dragged out of the house, burnt alive. There is no sign of his mother. In confusion and anguish he hides in a ditch for the night. Here he meets Astra who has broken her leg. He seems to recognise her but can't think where he has seen her before and she surprises him by knowing his name.

7.   Escape   33
Sebastian runs away from the town, deep into the forest, half carrying Astra. They eventually make it to a small clearing by a pool where Sebastian is able to heal Astra, using the knowledge and wax the wise old woman had given him.

8.   The Golden Ram   38
While lost in thought by the pool Astra and Sebastian see a Ram with a golden fleece enter the clearing. Astra encourages him over and he surprises Sebastian by talking to them. He invites them to come and meet his friends at a party he is having at his home. They willingly accept.

9.   The Ram's Tale   42
Our two heroes are whisked away to a snowy plateau at the very top of the highest mountain where they meet all the Ram's friends, a motley crew of Gryphons, Phoenixes and other mythical beasts who seem to be ghosts, fading away and dying. The Ram asks the heroes if they might be able to help them by bringing some water from the well that is at the centre of an island, which can be found in a lake beyond the Land of Ne'er Destroyed over the farthest western horizon. Astra and Sebastian excitedly accept and the Ram offers them some help in their quest by breaking off one of his horns and telling them, if they are ever in danger, to blow on it and he will be there in an instant. They are also to use the horn to carry the water home. Finally they all celebrate the brave heroes' decision with a huge party.

Astra and Sebastian

10.   The Chasm Challenge   50
Astra and Sebastian say goodbye to the Ram and head west, descending into a valley. As they proceed deeper and deeper the valley turns into a chasm that gets narrower and darker as the cliffs get higher. They are frightened and hold hands but soon get separated as Astra is distracted by a line of ants and sits down to rest leaving Sebastian to walk off alone.

11.   Siren's Bell   54
Sebastian, now alone, heads deeper into the chasm and hears a delightful voice whispering to him. This lovely voice soon becomes a crowd of beautiful women who nearly lure him into sexual congress. But, at the last minute, he remembers Astra and sees the angels turn into ugly crones who chase him as he escapes from the chasm through a tunnel in the cliff face.

12.   Astra's Journey   58
Astra, also alone, has fallen through an unstable floor into a tunnel. Lying there, semi-conscious, she is discovered and entranced by a beautiful prince who takes her up in his arms and carries her deep underground.

13.   The Bull Ring   60
Astra is carried to an altar in a pillared cavern underground and Sebastian suddenly arrives in the same cavern having run through a labyrinth of tunnels. The prince has now turned into a massive bull and is leaning over Astra to kiss her. Sebastian does battle with the Bull and kills him whilst Astra ties up in knots the crones who have followed him. As soon as these enemies are lying on the ground, beaten, the cavern starts to shake and collapse and the two heroes run hand in hand, through the only available exit, up a long path to daylight.

14.   On The Road   66
Our heroes emerge from the ground to glorious sunshine and see a road meandering generally west around hedges and fields. Each grabs the other's hand tighter and they follow the path, hoping to find the Land of Ne'er Destroyed. Soon their path is

Astra and Sebastian

blocked by a fearsome monster with two faces, one on either side of his head. The monster threatens them with death and separation but they talk to him gently and soon all end up dancing round in a circle. At the climax of the dance the monster gladly accepts his true form — that of a coyote — and they all fall into an exhausted sleep. When Astra and Sebastian awake the coyote has gone.

15.   Karkenios   73
It's the morning so Astra and Sebastian are getting hungry and head off up a hill, towards the west. When they reach the summit a magnificent view of a glistening glass city greets them, with the sea in the distance. They run down towards it and get some food from some strange silent merchants. They quickly ask questions as to why the town is so eerie but receive only a mysterious answer in the form of a plaque on the wall. Suddenly a bell is rung and everybody floods to the sea front, the two heroes going along with them.

16.   The Show   80
At the sea front the entire crowd is staring at a young girl tied to a cliff across the bay. She seems distressed so Sebastian and Astra, incensed, demand to know why she is tied up but are inadvertently forced into replacing her by a burly official, as they are strangers and making a fuss.

17.   The Crab   85
Astra and Sebastian, tied to the cliff, are suddenly confronted by a massive crab that bursts out of the water intent on eating them. They are swallowed by the crab and proceed to fight each their own way out. Once free Sebastian fights the crab to save himself from its angry pursuit and blinds her in one eye before swimming for the shore. As they approach the pier the ancient king of Karkenios commits suicide, jumping into the crab's awaiting claws. She then dives for the deep with the king inside her leaving Astra and Sebastian free in the sea.

Astra and Sebastian

18.   Drift   91
Astra and Sebastian begin to splash and play in the sea and this culminates in a kiss. They hug and float in the ocean and drift across the horizon where the sun is setting, finally arriving at a beach where a storm starts to build.

19.   Lion Trial   97
The storm rages and the palm trees lining the beach are struck by lightning. A gigantic lion emerges out of the flames and roars menacingly at them. Astra and Sebastian are struck dumb with fear, as the trees part revealing a stone circle in front of a magnificent temple which the lion seems to be guarding. The lion starts towards them and they run across the sand with the lion gaining on them at every step. They stumble and fall but, at the last moment, Sebastian asks Astra to blow on the Golden Ram's horn and suddenly the Ram appears with an army of his friends who defeat the lion. The storm recedes and our heroes take a breath. The Ram disappears.

20.   An Elemental Temple   104
The heroes, invigorated by their triumph, are drawn towards the magnificent temple. They are led through its seven gates by a serene voice which asks them to leave one item of their possessions at each of the gates until they stand naked before a pair of beautiful statues in the inner sanctum. They are welcomed to the centre of the universe and make love in the sand.

21.   Rising Up and Away   111
Our two heroes are whisked up to the stars to sit, one on each side of a set of cosmic scales, as king and queen of the universe. The two dishes of the scales are drawn up to the fulcrum and Astra and Sebastian are united as one being. They see the universe in all its infinite beauty, from the tiniest particle to a super massive star, from a black hole to the people on earth.

Astra and Sebastian

22.   The Land Of Ne'er Destroyed   115
The lovers awake to find themselves back on the beach, but the temple in front of them is now a ruin. They walk together through the rubble into nature and realise they have finally found the Land of Ne'er Destroyed. At its heart is a fantastical mountain with all of human history represented along a winding road that forms a concentric spiral up and down its sides. They follow the road and marvel at the story unfolding alongside them.

23.   A Floating Island   122
Astra and Sebastian complete their descent of the mountain of the Land of Ne'er Destroyed and walk past a scorpion to discover a lake with a mysterious island floating in the middle, just as the Ram had promised. They catch a boat to the island which turns out to be a beautiful woman lying on her back and spinning gently in a circle. Her navel is a well. From it they fill the Ram's horn with water, as the Ram requested, to take back to all those on the mountain as they had promised they would.

24.   A Magical Flight   126
The island Goddess rolls onto her side as the water is drawn and flings our heroes into the air. They are caught by a flaming arrow which carries them back to the mountain where the Ram is waiting for them with his friends all looking alive and well. He welcomes the heroes back and Sebastian hands him his horn full of water. He promptly places the horn back on its stub from which he had broken it to give to them at the very beginning of their journey and the water heals the wound but spills onto the ground. Sebastian is distraught after their epic journey for the water to be spilt but the Ram thanks them both and explains it has already done its job.

25.   The Return   130
The Golden Ram waves goodbye and a centaur leads Astra and Sebastian back down the mountain, through the forest, to the pool where they first met the ram all that time ago. Sebastian doesn't want to leave this magical place. To help him come to

Astra and Sebastian

terms with their return to their home, Astra talks to him about all they have learnt.

26. A New Age   **134**
Astra and Sebastian walk back towards the town and Sebastian excitedly talks of all the things he can't wait to show her. However, they don't find the town quite as they had left it. A massive road with cars speeding along it leads them to a sprawling city of towers and electric lights; there is a ruined castle in the centre of it all. The pair are stunned by this amazing place but are laughed at by the inhabitants because of their clothes, for they are still dressed as king and queen of the cosmos. Come nightfall they find themselves underneath a flyover, wondering what on earth to do. A tramp comes to their aid and tells them of a place where they will be made welcome. As directed, they go to the top floor of a nearby tower block where they are welcomed with tears of joy by Sebastian's mother and offered clothes, food and understanding people who want to hear their fantastic story.

Appendix: Brief Discussion of the Themes and   **150**
Symbolism in *Astra and Sebastian*

Early Responses to *Astra and Sebastian*   **158**

Illustrations
by Shelley Knowles-Dixon

Astra and Sebastian	Front Cover
The Ram's Tale	145
Astra emerging from the cave	146
Sebastian returns to find his home town burning	147
A Floating Island	148

Astra and Sebastian

*Sebastian and Astra kissed
And thus forever had begun*

Astra and Sebastian

Astra and Sebastian

1. THE CAVE

Beyond in days of mist and yore
There lived a girl a boy a story
Thunder's rumble lightening's glory
Rising stars and falling soldiers
Monsters to be faced and tested
Homesteads where a welcome rest is
Offered with an ale or two

Here in turn each drives the mill
To complement its spinning charm
Where folk and myth or legends born
Will gently ease the shaking arm

To truly taste a true beginning
Laud the call of venture's knell
And fly through stars illuminating
Castled shores and nature's spell

Stop by our sun the morning mist
Is burning off the day begins
And in a cave not far away
Our red haired elfin child awakes

This cave her hole her body whole
Set deep amidst the sloping hill
A time's lost countenance by rolling
Valleys flowers peaceful still

Sitting here she waits above the fires
Beyond the swaying gilded corn
Above the waving parapets
That can bear her weight no more

Astra and Sebastian

Forever looked beyond the wood
To find the one who might engage
Her love reveal her power release
The knower and the known on stage

For having not the path of blood
To alleviate her earthy maze
She donned a cloak complete with hood
And disappeared from earthly ways

Had barely touched fifteen years born
When cast abroad from fields of corn
Long castle walls which dominate
Our earthly plain and soul's dominion
By dictating through familiar
Schools of thought and people packed
Like apples waxed so's not to bruise

Denied the pride from new admirers
Her pretty face no place to fit
A mind more beautiful but there
Exists a wall of flesh and laughter
Where repeaters mimic art
As she was torn by living it

Today this morn the dawning sun
Doth tint the face with warmer hues
Reflecting that her time had come
The butterflies inside her flew

She pushed her hand the ground away
And strode to play past rocky outcrop
Egret's nest and mossy hillock
By the foxes in their banter

Astra and Sebastian

Walked the morning ran the day

Back to worlds where castles chorus
Ample hymns to cloudly porous
Phantom names on abstract thrones
Do be careful what you say

2. MEANWHILE IN THE MARKET

Hurry lad the market's fast
The myriad on muddied street
Crowd out the drawbridge move thy feet
Or with their wares they'll hustle past
This old portcullis first to meet
And marry profit's voluptuous daughter
Whilst we chew fat and lose our week

Sebastian the elder spoke
The father of the boy and yoke
Come stir thy soul lad mind the way
And point thy ego to the mud
For where he goes then so shall thee
Do stop these lofty dreams of blood
And drag yourself into today

As they passed through its arch and teeth
Above the gateway to the castle
Saintly faces of the patron
Halo walls of brick and mortar
Welcomed them with taxing eyes
Unto the wasp's nest
Purse strings tied

Astra and Sebastian

Boy one more time I catch you staring
Clip your ear and hold you fast
It's been awhile since those old fears
Have helped the lazy move their rear
You ain't heard that from me you hear

His bare feet tanned and mouth in rapture
The sun caught off his burnished hair
Hell why Sebastian so like your mother?
Well go on boy she's over there

For ever tragic beauty real
Her balanced waist beside the well
A feline grace not harmed replaced
By inner patience water bearer

How quickly though her vision parted
Sprightly smile caressed her face
With open arms she cleared the market
Only room for their embrace

He struggled thrice his age was telling
As she removed a grubby streak
And let him land kissing remarking
If you're so grown should earn your keep

He always came after his schooling
Today the weekend or the evening
Learning lessons from the living
As well as what is left or written

Willing bent in roughen clothes
To clasp both arms around his load
An earthenware pot spilling water

Astra and Sebastian

Whilst his mother long had practice
Sat the urn upon her hair

He followed her through doors and more
But never matched her shapely gait
Her hips a frame to elbow bent
A swaying painting done in taste

Sunk matted footsteps in the dust
That floored the inner castle space
And soaked the wet and excrement
From roaming animals throughout
And any careless men

They passed the master screaming wildly
A bard with but one string attached
A marble game young children playing
Wild hogs roasting on a flame

Sebastian learnt from his mother's
Doggèd choice to not attach
A moment's thought or heaven's voice
Onto the work of higher men

Where shadowed brow and creases doubt
If there is truth inside the mind
The whole existence of their pout
The first destruction of mankind

Alone the virtues of the mouth
Will heighten those the day debates
Reflect upon the separations
Sound will seek to couple up
Making thirst from lively talk

Astra and Sebastian

They grab a cup the same

The workers worked
The turning worm
Burnt muscle
Till the higher sun
Could bear no more
The horizon bit
And swallowed them
The day is done
And so are those with nothing won

The pitcher of their burden downed
They ceded to the subtle moon
That steeps an evening's dream with meaning
Keeping day within its form

And with the world back on her shoulders
His mother calmly led them home

3. HOME

Beside the fire her auburn hair
Caught every burnished wind and hue
That emigrated from the flame
To amplify the wooden room

The copper fat pot bubbling spat
She sighed and gently stroked his arm
I know you're tired but one last job
Won't ever harm a boy like you

He jumped up smart and called the dog in

Astra and Sebastian

Swept the day from off the floor
Made fast the door and thus secured
Their own position in the world

Then holding close
The candle he had made to last
Struck up a pose and sent her laughing
Acting stories once she'd spoken
From the bedside unto him

The play pen broke
Hey daddy's home
She laid a limb upon his arm
No skin was broke like from the father
As firm as oak with guile of willow
Yet a massive will evoked
He slowly checked his passioned tones
And took a book became remote

Stood heavy at the winter doorway
Sebastian the elder paused
Collecting from the firey warmth
All of his love for this his home

My Julia your beauty's much
I feel I miss your gentle grace
Come here to me a day's a wait
Of centuries whilst you're my mate

Their hug was done
The eyes unstuck
Hey boy I see you ruffled hair
Quoth next the grace
He took her place

Astra and Sebastian

Converting faces to the altar
An alcove tiny in the stone
A son a dog a wife a god
A silent family alone
Whilst he sent up their private prayer

Unclasped his hands discerned the plate
From nothing now is something gained
And picked a swathe of chewy mutton
For his dog drooling below

Then dropped his arm and peace was brokered
From his deer pelt jerkin flowed
A white clay pipe tobacco flattened
At his lips the smoke billowed

But clouds soon float out of the window
Marking fuller times of slumber
Sebastian in innocence
To those desires now churning round
The stomach louder
Born as hunger
Unfilled where adults keep awake
Until the elder urge is grounded
The oldest thirst we've ever known

At least she found the ecstasy
That only to the conjoined comes
Whole house as babes relaxed in wonder
At the dreams refused to none

4. A DAY OF KNIGHTS

Come the morn
At first he stumbled
To the door
Released his swollen bladder adding
Every day more foam to pool
In frothing wash against the wall

But not a day to marvel at this
Sign his head moves from the earth
For 'bove the hedge where streams the vista
Of the world he will inherit
Rises something tempting more

Today the boring golden corn
Is interspersed like a dew-tinged copse
With flashing silver
Over-layn by heavy gold

From pounding hooves
To panting eyes
The horses shod
With victory
Each mighty beast held back with leather
Steady reins draped rich with silk
The sword hilts golden silver armour

Above the blood
The helmet rang
Its visor sang
A marching tune
That amplified the
Ringing suit

Astra and Sebastian

Atop a cloth of harlequin
Heraldic saddles trumpeted
The emblem of their loyalty
Throughout the land

The noble deeds of troops untarnished
Called to gallop through a town
The oldest dream to save a darling
Free her land
And make it yours

His gaping mouth drunk on the scene
A quickening of valiant breath

When can I be dad
One day I will must be
More than ever more than death

But huskily his father sticking
Out his bearded agèd chin
Placed his hands upon the lad
And whispered knowingly

Hold your horses not too loud
The pain that lies outside our fold
Is one I hope you'll never see
For if you seek a time to fight
So you'll meet a time to flee
First list to me say that you will
Stay in your role your castle wall
Put family before it all
For whilst a calling is immortal
And their song rings heavenly
No man is better if he kills

Astra and Sebastian

Forever fettered in his freedom
Never settled or revealed

Sebastian now nodded rude
His head distilled
At once subdued
Uncomprehending
More confused by mute respect
A father talking over him

Ignoring thus the morning's promise
They all left to work or school
The household eye restored its patch
An earthy sod put on the fire
And softly shadowed door on latch

Sebastian to help the wild one
Chop her wood learn spells and roots
An earthen mother with no kindred
His earthly mother hoped would root
His life in skill and peaceful trade

Sebastian the elder left
His son to follow these distractions
Sullenly doubting there could be another
Path to choose than work or war
But keeping hope there could be more
He listened to his wife's persuasion
To the fields he took his sickle
And his dreams perhaps assured

5. WHICH WITCH IS WHICH

Ah there me boy you never are
Lame scurry quicker frogs plagued thou
He never knew quite what she said
Or why her voice lightened his plough

Her crinkled face and crooked grin
Dilapidated like her hut
The thatch on which was chattering
Together rippled windy touch

Soon wood was chopped
And herbs a-picked
He opened up his ears
A witch!
The other children chided itched
A hand that's held but wants to twitch
Will flick the switch of taunts to keep
From wishing they weren't incomplete

The wild old woman with no name
Or none not to his ears profane
Was Grammar to him for she liked
The subtle rules that life flows by

Hark as she beckons from the plain
And meagre door she must maintain
Come in dear child the sky turns thunder
Not much use you wet and cold
You may be strong and coming stronger
But by heaven don't rush to be old

Her simple broth was always filling

Astra and Sebastian

And delicious
Would you like a little more?
This ritual kept them both fulfilled
Giving has become receiving

She sat and puzzled the muddled weather
An afternoon of cauldron's tossing
Winds of change now and forever
Kept the silence wonder brings

It must be there for you to return
She finally revealed a yawn
For though the sun's not yet obscured
I've kept you longer than your chores

You take this bundle for your mother
And let him rub them on her shoulder
But keep this sweet you'll see reward
He took the sticky wax and promptly
Hid it deep within his shorts

Now make your tracks as creatures ought
He hugged her briefly through her warts
And ran through bracken rubble gorse

Surprised when she called sharply to him
Surreptitiously with age
Don't be obscured by all their rage
You make your way write your own page

He ran with youth above the rot
A sojourn higher than the word
Soon blesséd rain began to spot
This simple child and wetten him

Whilst spotted toadstools and the moss
Drank for life in huddled cover
Birds were silent for a change
As night not either sad or happy
Watched the storm tear through the wood

6. KEEP THE HOME FIRES BURNING

Emerging valiantly from the forest
The same old town but something changed

He blinked and ran on
Pushed through pasture
With a scream that lost to silence
All his effort was in vain
However much he moved their ears
The people stood
He didn't want to comprehend

Hot flame licked smoke fought with the rain
As all the fireflies in his brain
Danced off to die with falling truth
His body hovered on one foot
Disjointed from its path so posture
Took up root and moved no further

No more slumber only haunted
Owls and hues who've seen the ghost
Of more than they can understand
Removed from steady wood to land
On virgin branches over plans
Beyond all that which can be learnt
As silently he watched it burn

Astra and Sebastian

This one day late a piece of luck
How timeless notions have a touch
In that your soul not flesh is scorched
A spectre from a wooden door

His own before him
Creaking open
Through the porch
Ran two grown men with scorching feet
Forlornly dragging
Between them struggling
To lift the man and keep the form
The one that used to be his father
From sinking down into the ground

Of Julia there was no sign
But only darkness fire and flashes
Crashing beams and cracking bricks
Sebastian splashed back in darkness
Rigor mortis pinned him down
Refused to search or intervene
In case he lived beyond the dream
Consumed her memory to the fire
That night was blanketed with grief
A crushing orphan's pain

To his left roamed desolation
Chaos faces adult children
Shadows by the fire took turns
In shattered poses ice and burns
To spew and cry or throw a fit
Whilst other earthly chattels screamed
To shatter 'neath this change so wraught
By unkempt works a fractured force

Astra and Sebastian

That's where he lay no knight or mare
Could burn this daydream into darkness
Hard rain fell and dark smoke poured
Low anguished calls ravished the world
He quivered as the arrows soared
Grew colder as the sunrise poured
Ironic light into their pit

Within this cold despondant haze
Forgot himself and nearly stood on
A hooded girl he thought he'd seen
Or maybe dreamed of
Lain in sweat a broken leg

He stretched a hand for her to hold
This wretch that beamed where he was dim
On touching hands a cosmos shared
Sebastian knew his path was lit

Whilst she had found the one she craved
And that the boy had no idea
Of all the power within his core
But still he knew how to be brave
And hauled her out of there

We must get out
They're coming back
For o'er the hill rode
More attack
The romance gone
Its armour black
With torches lit
The smouldering
Ash captured embers

Flew to flame
He dragged her
Shouting
We must get out
The mad the smoke
No time for doubt

Sebastian

He choked his shout
She whispered pure
Ethereal sure
Yet taut with clout
It calmed him down

Though how she knew his name confused him
Behind the burning screaming shouts
Of misty morning's hardest binge
A father dead a mother burnt
A new-found friend
A world to learn
And him stuck in between

7. ESCAPE

During running
If she stumbed
He encouraged
If he mumbled
She encouraged
Never screaming
Simply dealing
With the world

Astra and Sebastian

And with her pain

Sebastian felt her hurt as much
As she felt all the stars they watched
Keep ebb and flow above their feet
And through each other felt complete

There came a pig and then a hut
Each maddened into raging forces
Desolate old children's voices
Sebastian
I'm Astra
Noises
Darkness
Causes
Father's dead
Your leg
This poison
How I know
She whispered
Darling
Blessings for your gentle touch
Your lighter feet
Enlightened deep
A wantless help
Will futures greet
No truer marvel
More complete

He turned his head
Her face obscured
By acrid smoke
Their eyes destroyed
Burnt faster than his acid muscles

Astra and Sebastian

Sturdy angels would've fallen

Instead their feet crushed calm old heather
Tangled as the two together
The sky glowing embarrassed red
Witness to the poorest weather

He knew of somewhere he could choose
A favourite place
Hidden retreat
Of light and pools and things to eat
Beyond the farthest bravest feet
Beside the smell of sweetest spring

Discovered when
Lifetimes before
He'd braved the long and nervous nights
And slept through thoughts of hidden claws
The noises tore him
Half asleep out in the wood
Exploring deeply as he could

Cheek to cheek not once they faltered
Heavy climbs were always countered
By a downslope second wind
That blew the smoke away from them

I'm sure it's here
I know although
It's been a while
Don't ramble please
She would cajole
It's really better if we go

Astra and Sebastian

A shortened breath a league or more
Until he gently eased her down
To let her sleep by hard wood fire
Beside a pond and teeming willow
An arbour for her dreams a pillow

On the rock was moss her blanket
All the ferns and dryer bracken
Grasses green as dew is wet
So easy worn by those who dare

Protected from the pressing stares
Of elements the shallow valley
Found the deepest congregation
Water flowers wind that asks
Before it dares to breathe on you

Amongst this deep and tranquil rest
In valleys blessed by fairies past
A flurry stirred the world that basked
A hardened breath that carried pain
He never asked but knew for sure
His witch had passed
No world the same
When one has left
Or somehow changed

Beyond in skies with smaller suns
Where thunder served a lightening tongue
The village turned against itself
And what was short is now thought long

Forced out the panic spread away
Into the wood before the day

Astra and Sebastian

The stealth that once had kept her safe
Now sent a vengeful stranger's death

Her thatch was burnt as crowds looked on
Silhouetted by the flame
Her screams were doused by sallow cheeks
Dishes brimmed with pain

The one that breaks clasps hands for friends
For one that falls another's pushed
And that once hot must so be cried for
Water on the burning bush

The brook mirrored the open sky
As each night passed the moon rose full
So still the world required no word
To tell all that he had to know
His real and known existence glowed

He watched her sleep in dripping clothes
The calm from bathing eased his woes
By tending what he cared the most for
Through his skills and older tincture
His witch lived on
The honey healed her
Water from the clearest pool
A certain flower picked at dawn
Made his reflections seem as real
As anything called to the fore

So as through days her body mended
He watched the fishes twirl together
Spiralling around the centre
Till the end with a flick of a tail

Astra and Sebastian

They swam away to start again

8. THE GOLDEN RAM

Their forest vale
   Moved with the moon
Her leg was healed
No longer lame
And fever gone
Yet still their bodies
Brimmed with pain

They wept for her they wept for him
For villages for lands for men
He for his parents and his witch
She for his scars that cut her deep
Assigned them each a star in heaven
May they shine within their sleep

On fish they fed and water drank
Through night and day and weather too
They never moved from on their bank
And probably like horses' glue
Would stick forever hooves unused

But as they mused across the clearing
Sidled in a skinny Ram
With tatty fur and cobbled kneeling
Bendy legs he dipped his head
A timeless moment more than thoughtful
Showed his proud inspiring horns
Whilst lapping at the placid water

Astra and Sebastian

Scraping up some grass for food
They both could tell an older power
Rested in this beast made rude
And used like autumn's seeded flower

Coaxing him with clicks and high voice
Sebastian sat
Whilst Astra stroked his weary coat
And whispered sugared compliments

From where my dear have you arrived
O tell me beast hast thou a name
The happy Ram soaked up her tidings
Bleated first then answered them

Why thank you child
I thought I'd vanished
It's been some time
Since humans noticed
My old passage round this globe
They call me Ram
The fire in sky
I've come from yonder
To pass by

Could we fail to notice you
Your golden coat
And massive horns
Will turn our heads
They're turning mine

All the while Sebastian
Sat on the side and tightly yawned
Discretely lost in pondering

Astra and Sebastian

If really he had heard it speak

You flatter me child
I've seen myself in yonder lake
Your peaceful eyes
Breathe poetry
Into an ancient wreck like me

Perhaps there's hope
I guess we'll see
He gave a whisper
To the whispering trees

So have you a home?
The Ram and Sebastian spoke at once
And laughed together
Forever friends

O my how rude
My name's Sebastian
My friend here's Astra
Our home was lost
To fire and war
The children sighed
As all the laughter passed and died

Then come you must
To mine at once
The ageing Ram
Grinned swung his head
For centuries now
I've roamed at will
Just seeking but the simple chance
To show nay truly introduce

Astra and Sebastian

All my old friends
To someone new
And throw a party
Have a dance

A checking glance sent to the other
They smiled and shrugged
Why certainly
Then scrabbling the children stood
A party that sounds rather good
You've been much better company
Than most we've had here recently
And now we've cried should leave the wood
To get back on with life for good

Well jump aboard
The proud ram roared
Gaining strength from every touch

They clambered up
And skittered wildly round the lake
Behind them hoofprints in the mud
Before them dreams of true escape

A sower's wind blew out their cheeks
They whooped and grinned
Looping the lake
A forest path took them away
To feral dancing in the sun

Astra and Sebastian

9. THE RAM'S TALE

They hugged and tugged the golden fleece
Whilst galloping through warm charmed pastures
Fabled hills and valleys hidden
Copses trees and rivers bid them
Morning waving gentle laughter

The great Ram's horns invited probing
He touched them as the trees rushed past
She gripped on tight was too entranced
With flashing springs and nature's dance
For two days clear and without halter
They all ran on a cosmic dancer

Till out the forest they emerged
To wind and breeze and distant birds
The water fell away below
And fragrant air got thin to blow

They climbed a twisting rocky path
That with the Ram's fleet hooves felt easy
Ground was sparse then softer snow
And dappled cold but never freezing

The flat plateau at the farthest high
Sloped proud against the mountain line
So beautiful amongst the stars
Where time forgets you must come down

Their rampant Ram stopped here and ploughed
A loose furrow into the snow
Then turned to them with blinding eyes
And smiled

Astra and Sebastian

My children
Here's my home

The excited pair saw bright reflections
A cloudless sun eased blue from white
And all around the snow on snow
Did softly offer calm direction
Many feet had trod this plain
Connecting tracks on earth to sky

The Ram he led them seemed to grow
His bass voice deep a gentle bellow
To tell the truth I need to show you
Who I think that you should know

Approaching cautious from all sides
Came monsters that to fearful minds
Would quite disturb an earthly night
But in the light of balanced sight
And with a solid introduction
Become close friends and confidants

The children smiled and tried to focus
But then each creature lost position
Separating in the breeze
That silky edge of wetted leaves
Where truth remains an apparition
Trapped in human box shaped dreams

A phoenix flew
Her tale was told
A dragon blew out curling smoke
Around the northern star he floated
Before becoming as remote

Astra and Sebastian

As monuments we now discard

A gryphon on a far flung rock
Curled its gnarled neck
Read aloud
From an old bound book
Heavy leather
Showing dark against the snow

Then strolling 'cross the wide plateau
A slow precession of mythic beasts
All heroes villains to and fro
The cosmic cycles we complete

Below the mount the atmosphere
A brittle shell that phosphoresced
Beneath a glorious burning sun
Now coalesced the ghostly long
Procession into humming song
Of faces when imagination
Wants to tell articulate
How it should feel to be awake

The party twirling
Raptured full reverberating
Sebastian and Astra whirling
As the Ram began to speak

Behold this land behold its thirst
It's oft avoided seeming cursed
But still exists in thoughts of old
And tales of new yet to be told

Look at the edges of your earth

Astra and Sebastian

Where day and night are once begun
Makes one man smile another smirk
As we in turn back up your sun

Above your earth we live our game
Yet all restricted to this plain
A lifeless equilibrium
Once fed by fire and tidal waves
That now have flattened to a sigh

From here we would descend and play
Within your realms of fur and scale
Now only I go summoning
The will of all those waiting here
In hope that we might breathe again

For now we're seen to make life worse
Suggesting something more than earth
You see our beaten brow and fur
All matted mangy boney showing
Ghostly waifs the colour faded
Yellowed pages pressed like flowers
Flattened bled and then ignored

We're dying lost
And vanishing
Old faded ghosts
Hewn onto trinkets
Reinstate
Simplicity
Come share our story
To be free
Internment
Isolation means

Astra and Sebastian

The banishment of every soul
A death that keeps you living glory
Is a pain worse than a scream

You two can help us I implore
For are the first since times of yore
With open eyes that see beyond
A simple physical description
Pulling on the stellar plough
Includes a circumnavigation

Sebastian the first to yell
What are we simple folk to do

The crowd to standstill
Dancing stopped
His echo flew
And coming round
Uncomfortably grew

Then silence hung as silence should
A vestal robe for contemplation
Shifting hooves patted the snow
As wings ruffled anticipation

The Ram exhaled
Articulated
If wisdom comes quick to a child
Who will believe not be denied
Or prove they know to be alive
To grow is not lose this side
For in the centre far from here
The centre of it all my dears
Beyond the Land of Ne'er Destroyed

Astra and Sebastian

Beyond the scale
Beyond it all
An island spins she lies asleep
The mother of the first and end
Her navel is the flaming well
Dug deeper than the oldest longing
Can you draw the sweetest water
Bring to us her only daughter
Resolute beginning

The Ram now paused for was his turn
In nervousness at being seen
To be as nervous as he seemed
His mane curled up in knots

The task in hand the quest expounded
Sebastian and Astra calmly
Stared beyond the open sky
Then turned to eye the other grounded
Smiled again
And sounded gleeful
Hey for sure
You're on! We're in!

The sun flared up the cosmos brighter
The softest wind became a song
Please let yourselves believe in us
As much as we believe in you

The Ram smiled back
Fortuitous luck
Is yours in turn
For though we'll help you
Understand

Astra and Sebastian

We must be asked into your land
That's harder than you think
Young man

Sebastian took up the reins
The fire inside his heart aflame
Now that you've told us where to go
We'll do good by you fill the flask
Just help us now don't offer promise
Where exactly is this place

Whoa there young sir not simple truths
All I can do is point your face
For true direction beyond youth
Is yours to find and find that place

Look at me boy he shouted stamped
Sebastian his eyes were damp
To get thee far you need a lamp
To get thee home you need a map

All I can show you is that forwards
Lies the route to certainty
Beyond this crowd
He raised his hoof up
Walk along the rising sun
Till called back round
Then you'll have surfaced
By completing every cycle
We venture on Astra declared
We'll find your land I know it's there

Then in reply from worlds beyond
The Ram bellowed an animal prayer

Astra and Sebastian

To fill the nerves of everywhere
With love of fear a curious song
That makes you feel alive aware

Now both the children filled with zeal
Did silently begin to kneel
To ask themselves for farther truth
To ask as much of them as you

Awakened from their thought felt pause
The Ram soon quietly expounded
Not only whim can I bestow
But give you substance for your quest

Before their unsuspecting eyes
Before one could react and stop him
Our sun blessed Ram
Broke down and snapped
A wholly real
Benevolence
One horn from on his holy brow
He placed it in their silent hands
The change from simple offering
To giving as the source of change

All weakly staring at the stub
The breath from each a shallow grave
The Ram whispered you fill this up
When 'tis you find the realm of light
And too if trouble bends you down
I'm tough enough to hear your call
If through this hollow horn you blow
Then any of us gathered beasts
Will suddenly be by your side

Astra and Sebastian

A cord was sourced he tied it true
Onto his back viewed lands afresh
Sebastian had visibly grown
Had noticed Astra's comely flesh
Much rounder had a gentle curve
Than what he thought he'd seen before
He blew the horn to sound their nerves
And put his thoughts to what's ignored

The horny note ran wide and true
And all the wanting ears responded
Made as one they tinged the dark
A family of branched extension
All to be our own complexion
Vivid colours faded out
The old sunset's paternity

Then through the night as stars looked down
They bore witness to quite a party
Celebrations loudly raucous
Humans and creatures
Who live in their thoughts
All came together danced and talked
And filled the land with laughter

10. THE CHASM CHALLENGE

In the morning with the sun
Our children warmly hugged their Ram
Then boldly struck out through his land
The massing ranks that now were fading
Turning back to flakes of snow

Astra and Sebastian

Too soon the Ram was dim and distant
Like the silent snow a figment
Of a long fragmented past
The land dipped down became a valley
Away from myth and clouds now human
Forests shrouded overcast

Sebastian he stopped just then
But for a second to check his pack
Then running catching her descent
Found our Astra holding back

Like this the pair of them descended
Hopping inter stopping hearts
Not looking back or walking forwards
Faster than momentum forced

Nor did the view provide much comfort
Trees and trees and between them black
To where the distance fell away
One second marking many hours
Minutes melting into days

Through darkness nests and messy bramble
Our hero pair descended deeper
Touching leaves 'till out again
Whilst all the time the slope fell steeper

Sought no more than squeezing harder
Hands declaring what is fact
And so the two of them together
Kept progressing forth intact

Across the valley's rock and boulders

Astra and Sebastian

Foaming mouths of dragons weep
And then they saw its maw and whimpered
One dark canyon delving deep
Into the real descending night
The valley cliffs grew steeper darker
Dug their heels in for the fight

The curving path became a track
Its way unwound a steady river
Onto darkness into black
This chasm nest closed off the heavens
Left one star above the cliffs
A letter in the inky tract

Their eyes adjusting to the fact
Can only see what makes a move
But when all's settled we relax
She stopped he walked
Their contact broken
Matter fact alone

This canyon's trap referred them back
To colder climes before life dreamt
To unify their discontent
When sight and senses furnished only
Lonely ends and foetal farms
And not the hearts that beat between

A line of ants had claimed her interest
Liquid red the brightest sight
She knelt and wholly soul invested
Mind into distraction's plight

Although perhaps required a moment

Astra and Sebastian

Alone to watch relax and focus
She saw Sebastian making tracks
But never thought to shout or show off
Stop him reunite their act

But nor he felt to once look back
His head for skies lost heart was trapped
In everything he thought he wanted
And crouching down she couldn't know
Or with his dilate eyes make peace
Her view a swaying head and back
She cried O how is it that he can leave

When sitting down her world dismantled
So the ground beneath her cracked
A fissure tearing up the ground
Where once had marched sure and securely
The extended arm of the army of ants
She fell and floated down the crack

Her hollow chest
Of empty breath
Coughed as she fell
Through fester freed
The mottled dance
Of breezy billowing
Swirling dusty ancient air

Till landing in an underground chamber
Smacks and cracks her body ached
As rocks and ground now hit her back
As hard as she had hit them

11. SIREN'S BELL

All the while that Astra stopped
Sebastian walked on gentle feet
The relic of a surer plan
That somehow seemed far out of reach

Caught in the thrall of this underpass
Where demon wraiths add weight to air
Unsteady cliffs their sides a mask
For tremulous uncertainty

But Hark!
A voice calls through the dark
O Breth-er-en. … Boy Breth-er-en

A sound that's brighter than the stars
Which gaily pock mark heaven's face
When in the space of open life
Outside the confines of this strife

There came a light at first a glow
Then radiance a softer halo
Flooding warm unearthly tone
A truce to capture those alone

With fingers glowing red translucent
Shielding fronds before his eyes
Drew up his knees to run and dive
Away from this predicament

O Bretheren Boy Bretheren

Be welcome dear a traveller lost

Astra and Sebastian

Is never far from true redemption
Do not falter rest on moss
Share my breath as one who must

And then he saw her face beneath
The wrappings of this sonic cloak
A fresh visage of youthful past
Her beauty deep surreal remote
Sebastian drew out a sigh
The first wisp of her soul evoked

Now captivated watched this ghost
Across the insurmountable void
That can exist between a pair
Of human forms
If hidden there
A doubt of true connection shared

Soon both lost souls were reaching forth
Like remembering angels touching palms
The gorge was filled with elated rainbows
Summers breeze and hearfelt charms

Yet as he made the final step
Between the darkness and the rose
His fears of bliss inert were versed
The promised void was sharp with thorn
Made fast to stop his front foot falter
Panic'd like a horse in halter

For he'd a partner wasn't solo
And she should share this finest hour
In vain he looked beyond the halo
Found but darkness felt more trapped

Astra and Sebastian

He strained for Astra over wind
Then heard a sound like falling plaster
As silence broke to pressing laughter
A crowd of angels drowning him

Astride the horizon of events
Just by the corner of his eye
The strongest wrongness amplified
Her honeyed face broke into rattles
Colder cheeks and hoarser cackles
Fragile eyes turned to demands
His angel aged but caught her anger
Turning to a charming patter
Relaxed her face retrieved its smile
Replaced the grace within her guile

O Come my love my missing one
'Tis timeless where the day is done

Enough enough
Backed to the cliff
He watched these visions grab and circle
Flashing changing changeling stiffs
A crone a wraith a wraith a crone
A maiden coming forth to hug him
Rosy cheeks and wetted lips

A chattel broke and siren bells
Were clanging in Sebastian's brow
All youthful innocence dismayed
At witnessing this cloying mass
Of hags intent to cut his wrists
To grasp and grope his every part
With hit and fist envelop art

Astra and Sebastian

In one quick breath he dove for freedom
Beyond the first one of the song
Who smiling sweetly checked his arm
But pushing strong burst on through all of
Them that sought to halt escape
His pupils grew and darkness sparkled
Saw a tunnel in the wall

The way to break this chasm's coil
Was diving deeper 'neath the soil
His footsteps rang off vaulted rooves
The bricks and soil and twisted roots
Passed on to him their cackled threats
We've got him girls he's but a youth
Will surely fall for all our troupe

You have me wrong
Sebastian
Counts one to
Pandemonium
I am a man
This capture is your childish dream
You'll not transfer
Its loss to me

He kept on sprinting
Dashing down
The descending ground
A pleasant grace
By which he floated
Over stone
Fallen debris
And rivulets
Those mini moats

Of castles built for mice
It seems

Not once confused by consciously noticing
The million pathways of the maze
Or putting any marker down
For going back was not allowed
So why consider it

12. ASTRA'S JOURNEY

A similar fate was hers to follow
But not to know as first on waking
A vision formed one handsome man
Amidst the fug dank smell of rats
That rankled wrinkled up her face
And sent a shiver down her back

Then sweetly as her nose relaxed
The heavy bass notes eased her back
Its tincture stroked her hair a mat
Upon the sharp rocks calmed attacks
Of alto sighs goosebumps on skin
A palace kept remote to her
Had now begun to settle in

Vibrations grew until she knew
With open eyes he stared at her
Extending arms to wrap her glue
Her to his manly chest and brush
Away the dust
So she could nestle in his hair

Astra and Sebastian

Sweet Astra gazed into his eyes
And then beyond to yonder skies
Where twinkling through the roof top hole
The dazzling spark of one true star
His hand was young but still felt old
She felt secure in that

You're beautiful the man exhaled
As she inhaled his every word
No other gift could grace as much
These tunnels closed to rush of blood
And pounding hearts for countless years
A bondaged heart's but free to curse
So now I bless your countenance
And flourish with a new found verse

He never let her walk and so
For every mazey tunnel turn
Through having nowhere else to go
Young Astra fell into his charms
And cuddled in his glowing arms

His lacquered dripping gentle babble
Mixed with moss and water channels
Painted rocks shone with enamel
Phosphoresced or milky white
Were silent but for stalactites
Which dripped their water into light
Enamoured mites hear this as bells
Like Astra floating in her spell

The muscles taut within his arms
Seemed less to cage than to disarm
Unpeel her stress and chime her charms

Forgot about Sebastian
The ants and stars
Became as one
A memory
The deeper deeper that she fell

13. THE BULL RING

Sebastian he ran away
Whilst she was walked to servitude
So both were trapped inside the maze
Now marking out an equal path
For though the boy a shorter leg
He numbered more
Than the longer tread
Of her tall prince
Within whose arms she rode

Thus with each step
To Sebastian's many
The ignorant racers drew together
Deep inside the heart of earth

The charming prince
Had reached his goal
And laid her down
All keen and ready
She unconscious
And unsteady
Unequivocally a lady
In the wrong part of the town

They'd found a courtyard

Astra and Sebastian

Underground
A circle pillared
Paved and round
Where still she lay
In foetal comfort
On a cold damp
Granite table

Her arms draped down
Its sides of stone
Vague mind disabled
Body coiled
The prince he poised
Dipped to her mouth
The dripping ceiling
Painting moisture
On her lips
But without potent inflammation
Was not as he would like to think
All wet through long anticipation

A broken kiss
As crashes sounded
Of the sharpest
Clarifying
Heart stopped mighty
Shouting sounds
The pounding feet
Of chase or rescue
Echoing about the gloom

The water turned to blood her mouth
A steely taste
Her blue eyes saw

Astra and Sebastian

With gaze aghast
She kicked him in the pelvis
Laughed

Sebastian dumb struck was pressed
Like Samson trapped between two pillars
Another hidden entranceway
But one of twelve around the junction
The ancient courtyard where she lay
Could not believe what he was seeing
A massive Bull clutching himself
Whilst looming over his princess

Sebastian let out a roar
Together they each saw the truth
His hers this maze the cloven hoof

The dripping sweat her eyelids butter
Heart engorged enraged with blood
She muttered fiend a hiss of steam
Escaped her lips she rolled uncluttered
Off the altared white stone chipped
Onto the reddened muddy floor
All clotted blood dripped off the walls

A broken spell
Sebastian charged
She understood
The merry wives who followed him
Were agèd crones with faded jaws
And soggy breasts no babies clawing
Sought to suckle save their mourning
Circumvent the inevitable
The invisible shifting mortal coil

Astra and Sebastian

From taking them to further toil

In turn she dove to scatter them
And tied their white and weary tresses
Into knots a mess of wonder
Twisting faces to distresses
Eye to eye their sorrow mounted
Cursing others fell asunder
A lake of fabric in the mud

Then Astra ran and trampled them
Which dashed their hopes rising again
The petty prayers of pretty girls
Worked into bones
Torn from the world
Then tied to husbands
And a home

The pawing hooves of the bull alarmed
Beat heavy on the muddy ground
His great horns swung to gore the forces
Faced delusion now much more

For blood rushed from a gaping wound
A gash opened his jugular
Inflicted by Sebastian
His hungry anger found release
And focused on this torrid beast

Although less weight
And shorter height
He had the future
In his sight
Beneath the horns

Astra and Sebastian

He reached and spied
The apple he had been denied

Embraced the stretch of his pent up yawn
With crashing teeth of the younger man
Now grown to know his fatal dawn
He took the air himself
And gnawed
Through fur and sinew
Blood and gore
Until it pawed at breathless air
And felt the floor
Its granite grave

The Bull collapsed
The beast released
Sebastian's demented joy
Stood on the altar
Raised his arms
Surveying all that lay before him
Any more to be destroyed

The walls beat him their master void
And with a hiss began descending
To join the mess left on the floor
Saw crashing mortar smelt the hell's scent
Brimstone ash salt-petre air rent

Finger tip on pursing lip
She fixed her finest look on him
Before the fire the dust the din
One hand on hip
He woke from pride
Sent her a grin

Astra and Sebastian

Where hands once shaking
Now were still

Jumped swiftly down
From up on high
Hands clasping hers
Pulled them together
Returning to the fable grown
Within the shiver of a hug between
Two future lovers
Set the scene

The circle's side was spiralling
As minerals offered a ghoulish glow
The courtyard swiftly closing in
From one vast ocean of dimly lit pillars
Onto this tiny focused spot
They dived for life
And worried not

Together danced to the only hole
The final exit tall and wide
Each freakish bride their horror husband
Were crushed behind as all the walls
Closed finally like hungry jaws
Grasping for young virgin shores
The tunnel crashing down behind

With rushing breath
And scraping shoulders
Up they ran to meet the stars
Through twisting tunnels
Stepping bolder
Outpaced all the dashing mess

To burst exultant to the sun

Each could not relinquish their grip
On the other's
Hot and gentle special hand
As silently the land reclaimed
Its oldest maze
The childish cave of castled days
Whilst valiantly the sun shone on
The noble land of inquiry

14. ON THE ROAD

Behold the east the new horizon
Turn away or try and face me
Although you maybe see a face
You'll never see the whole of me

The voice of questing wind still whispered
Nothing's won by separation
So linking arms they walked as one
Throwing seeds into the wind
And basking in the golden threads
Hot molten rays the youngest sun

The boy was older and the girl
Had grown by actions underground
But neither had yet come to know
The turbulence of temper's wand
That open air of tenderness
Found swimming deep in love's embrace
Beneath light covers outside clothes

Astra and Sebastian

A dream without a unique face
Duality could wander on

The road ahead was old and cornered
Pastures fields where hedges flowed
Around the edges crows would laugh
They twisted corners on a path
Which gently bore their weight along to
The dawn of something beautiful

The grey stone true had depths within
For underfoot it felt like water
A blessing left to float in skin
As nature's son and heaven's daughter

They passed a blissful day or more
Some warming nights in heather beds
Till suddenly the hedges browned
Cacophony replacing sound

Around a bend both lovers stopped
Fixed by the sudden jolt of shock
The road was blocked a gruesome stranger
Glared at them with scorn and danger

First its foul face drew in their stare
A nightmare diabolical
Tall black top hat its face beneath
Had sharper eyes than any pin

Black suit bedecked with conduits
A clock some string a reel a stick
He turned around the hat now checked
Not plain with red and white was flecked

Astra and Sebastian

A strange new face leered hard at them
A simple suit of white linen

The two faced one man
Spat out flame
And soon was clear why all the mire
Why blackened hedges
Human trails
And human trials
Blunt undermined
By louder tantrums
From this tyrant strangled twin

The pain of unexpected change
Or pure destruction and rebirth
The two as one the one is two
A tide unchecked will drown the lakes
A forest fire gives seeds a break

It roared
They froze
But never trembled
Fire flew past their shoulder blades
The heat flushed red into their cheeks
And yet our couple bravely hailed him

Howdy stanger what's the muddle
May we pass our journeys longer
Than this road
A distance double
Can't you see we mean no trouble
Just another day to be

But aren't you scared to see yourselves?

Astra and Sebastian

Half his heart spoke
Whilst cackling with indecision
So his question left a bump
Upon the flat horizon line

Sebastian and Astra spoke
Without committing any lie
We're not yet sure if I is carved
Into a stone
Beyond the ancient alphabet

The two faced thing
Span on its axis
Now a black hat
Stared at them

Uncertainty will be your fall
As you must choose
The vile or gentle?
Less or more?

Again the same the answer's all
For on the spot your question's void

Do you feel hot
Or cold as fact?
Attack or wait?
The checked hat back
Its dam near bursting
Questions sounding more like curses
They never thought how to respond

We're scared yet strong
Some right some wrong

Astra and Sebastian

Like lightening's noise
Is gorse aflame
A meal not more
Than we can claim
Or plain discourse
That moves like tides
First in then out
As never can one be forever
Or forever be at once
We're like our sun breaking the heavens
Hot imperfect utter nonsense
To all leading moral questions

Before your feet the tricker teased them
Lies a quicksand that'll eat you
If you dare to question me
Or try to pass by force or please
Of this I'm sure so hold your crease
And do not try to call the run

But eye to eye they moved in closer
Against the prevalence of danger
And safety theirs the path was sure
Each step was steady never floored

They circled it
This thing
Connected
Were their arms
A golden ring
All spinning round
And loudly singing
Made the creature frown
And question

Astra and Sebastian

Them more brashly
In defence

Tell me of life
What what am I?
Dare contend me
With your mind
I'm good or evil
You decide

But are you either they replied
For only your judgements will haunt you and time
You're never worse than cold or hot
A cough or what you meant to say
Laughter changes your complexion
It's never what you ask or not
But do you need an answer got
That won't provoke another question

O my you want to play with me
I cannot harm a soul that's free
He finally joined in with their dance
The trickster twirling
Spinning round

When his two faces passed their eyes
Became as one within the spin
Sometimes I take from them belongings
As that was taken away from me

The more it danced
Became complete
Accepted in a place agreed
For something new must first have seed

Astra and Sebastian

And something to make way or heed

They saw its face complete a whole
Twisting spinning dervishly
No longer strange or as a stranger
He formed the promise of a smile

With flashing eyes
Dropped to all fours
And changed his form
A young coyote
Barking loudly
Chased his tail
And ran some more

Alive our life seems full to bloom
And now the night is seeing stars
The leaves themselves are edged with dew
A corona to the hope of you
The changing taste of certainty
A nod to opposites in truth
So Astra thought whilst spinning gaily
If I could say but what I do

Sebastian felt the force as well
Now truly accepting the dusk of youth
What's left unsaid can keep the spell
Alive without the need of proof

As they began to separate
The first I've met
The breathless dog
Gasped happily
His face as red as deciduous forests

Astra and Sebastian

With jumps of joy awaiting spring
His flapping tongue
Out tasting freedom
That simply takes me as I am

Sebastian smiled wearily
I'm tired he yawned
Astra agreed
Reposed upon the growing lawn of
Verdant springing greenery
Each individual blade of grass
Composed with all in sympathy
Neat movements in the symphony

The young coyote
Ran around
And playfully
Eroded ground
As his two guests
Well earnt their rest
Slept easily and peacefully
Quite gentle in each others arms
Whilst through the night the trickster smiled
And chased his tail some more

15. KARKENIOS

The road was long the route unplanned
The days wore like abrasive sand
On their bare feet soft way back when
Grew calloused as the skin gets thick
As too the mind from focusing
And nothing more becomes annoyed

Astra and Sebastian

How far away is Ne'er Destroyed

One night they lay without a shawl
Was thinking mused Sebastian
Should we have asked that mad coyote
Where's this place we're looking for

Poor Astra sighed grown late the hour
And long the stem of answer's flower
But he'd a challenge far too much
For us to think of day to day
Trapped in the midst of mud and string
We helped him move he helped us see
Beyond the wood we knew already
Onto deeper forestry

Then bright and early when the sun
Relieved them from their solid sleep
The moon had run another course
And so the next month had begun
As well as a new day of course

They both rose quick
For hungry now
And felt the pull of deep hid thicket
We'll find some food
Sebastian mused
Not through the noisy morning crickets
Our prudence is a finer fellow
Playing with the fairer whim
We'll smell our figure head up wind

They laughed and breathed
Refreshed by sleep

Astra and Sebastian

Ran 'gainst the breeze
Which fluttered leaves
On supple trees beside the road

Into the dawn
The eastern morn
They jogged along
The road was flat
Then up a hill
Walked slower
Slowing every stride
And deeper drawing breath inside
The top drew near
Decayed to standstill
Time caught up
Then like a bounding pendulum
The maximum aspect of change
Arrived the moment that they stopped

Velociraptor
Hungry eyes
Now saw as clear
A vaster wish
Than just a dish
The vista of a splendid city
Spreading out to farthest shores

The gleaming sun now high and proud
Was glinting off a Ziggurat
And plains of glass surrounding it
In a valley spreading out

With parks and spires
Tall ships and halls

Astra and Sebastian

A destination to aspire to
Destiny within its thrall
Its walls squared up to classic fountains
Streets and bricks and something more

The pyramid beyond a symbol
Of the power that humans form
A station with vibrating quartz
A shining laser streaming out
From in its belly through a tunnel
Refecting mirrors in the sky
Were raised by older generations
Than the houses it obscured
A vision of the greater score
A choir led by a solo voice

Surreal for at this distance tranquil
Few sounds rode amongst the breeze
As down the hill they ran to feel
And feed off people and a meal

Towards this city built on light
They slid and tumbled
Reaching cobbles
Running yonder
Down a street
Then up another
To the centre
Buildings taller
Monuments
Of whiter marble
High walls
High rise
People dense and

Astra and Sebastian

Occupied
But not so every sense improved
The gutter grew a darker brown

The people crossing cobbled roads
Wore headdresses robes of white
Where patient horses heavy halter
Seemed to pull without a problem
Chariots of gold and fire

We're here they cried
The very centre of this town
The massive Ziggurat looked down
As their cry rang off silent glass
Reflecting round and round the square

Though magic here was everywhere
Excited and confused they stared
At buildings first they saw themselves
Then focused through beyond the wall

Where all's bizarre not market hall
For though the people traded chewed
And other things that people do
No one spoke just crystal gleaming
People working in a dream
A vision of success

This deadly calm seemed to be learnt
A smile that's smirked to cover up
A curse or worse the guilt of one
The population like a corpse
At once felt close and yet remote

Astra and Sebastian

Too much to move all their feet floated
Over pavements or the saddle
Sebastian and Astra entered
Through a door onto a concourse
Where were lined up rows of shops

Thinking they don't know the language
Food was sourced with smiles and charm
Which rippled back from mirrored traders
Bright and sharp always the same grin
Staring at these cheerful children

They only stared but never asked
Where might these travellers have come from
Impatience made Sebastian bold
And through a mouthful of their sweet bread
Spluttered crumbs and asked the name

Graceful heads snapped round and stopped
Once placid eyes astonished bored
A gaze so hot Sebastian shifted
From his spot and checked his arm

Then rising like an occult breath
A wave of sound rushed through the hall
But disappeared 'fore loud enough
To know it had been there at all

We name
Our town
Karkenios
Karkenios
We name
This town

Astra and Sebastian

A whisper from the growing crowd

Encouraged by this gentle sound
A formal circle drew around
Was outlined by the curious
But coloured by lament

Then Astra asked
Don't you ever speak properly
Scratch your knee or release some gas
Now I know you understand us
The silence is unnerving me

The silent troupe
Prepared a smile
And pointed to a plaque up high
Cast bronze upon the glassy wall

The sun of suns has shone for us
And we give thanks to flowered light
Thus living forever forever to rule
Over the dreaded night

For why have need of loud disruption
Pike or argument corruption
When each colour has a function
How we complement each other

Giving them their piece of fate
We'll surely keep the bay at bay
A triumph over entropy
Appliances over debate

For what is more than one eon

To live beyond resuscitation
Fortune blesses what we are
And all we have is golden

Even the silence
Sebastian muttered
As more and more chariots
Sped by without clatter

But who is the enemy to demand such a tax
And what a high price for just more years of life
For what can you do with all of this time
Success might be fine but there's far finer things
To occupy time 'til it comes to the end

The cobbles slapped the soles of their feet
As they walked off together

16. THE SHOW

The silence peaked
A long horn blasted
All the people
Started rushing
Another gong
Clang chaos formed
As tools were downed
The trades departed
From their foothold
In the market

Astra moved off with the beat
Sebastian fixed to her heel

Astra and Sebastian

Through corners steep
At crossroad streets
They kept momentum
Downhill rolling
Through the crowds
Of floating feet
Till finally
They found the harbour
Water front
Tall ships and lights
And something darker
The crowd around
Stalled promenade
Were staring out
At cliffs away
Across the bay
Where something strange
Was standing out

They joined the masses straining necks
And shielding eyes against the sun
A tiny speck became the focus
Of all the horde and swarming fuss

Beyond the waves beneath the sun
A pained and painted face was flush
Her flowing locks and demure hands
Were beautiful a teenage maid
Was reaching out to milk the land
For her lost freedom fair release

Her pain was plain
Chained onto rocks
But not from blame

Astra and Sebastian

Just who she was

You saw this in her silent plea
And from the perverse sniffs of pleasure
Ricocheting through the crowd
Voyeurs watching feeling shame

Sebastian turned to his neighbour
Just to check what he'd deduced
Be still she whispered
Took his arm
We must get closer
Try to understand the charm

They mustn't harm her
Charged Sebastian
The sky groans without lighter dress
The sea is blackened by distresses
Over farmed and dangerous
We've seen beneath their glory show
This dam must burst before we go

Through all the crowds
Through barricades
They slipped and pushed
Soon at the front
Where larger waves
Were close the breakers
People stared
And turned on them
Unwanted strangers
Only getting in the way

From feeling the slur of ambiguous eyes

Astra and Sebastian

Sebastian forced himself to try
For one last time
Go ask again
An armoured guard
Who stood watching the scene nearby

The question caught him by surprise
His armour shook
With laughter at an innocence
Mistaken here for ignorance
But only by the ignorant

He arrogantly flexed the talons of knowledge
A tower locked fat bunch of keys
She's not alive dead by decree
No more alive than Gorgon's sea
Which we appease but once a year
Why so surprised what more to see
For suddenly Astra had shied
Away from such a glorious spree

We cannot let your law be passed
It's out of phase by some degree
How can you think you have control
Over your age or any sea
A harbour's shallow
But the wider ocean's free
It's gone too far ridiculous
You first must listen if to see

Then tactful Astra squeezed Sebastian
Pulling him beyond the guard
Whose eyes took on strange looks of knowing
Harder than they'd ever seen

Astra and Sebastian

A certainty that only grows when
Everything forgets to breathe

Don't push boys
Now where are you going
He firmly grabbed them by the hair
An audience must pay its way in
I've found a way that you can save her
Let her work again

Their hope lasted but two of his strides
For quickly whisked faster than tides
Out to the cliffs the edgy road
Of gulls and lamps that tempt the boats
And shadows easily confused
With coats and coasts and all that's real

He doesn't mean
He bloody does
Sebastian knew that Astra knew
But had to vocalise

Just then the cracking public system
Gave address across the crowd
A bard with house and mouths to feed
Can only write what he's allowed

Two strangers young
Fit for our task
Insult the wit of elders past
Now volunteer
Redeem themselves
And help us pass this greatest day
Without a loss in population

Two small drops into the ocean
Make a splash for us today
So give them up a great hooray

17. THE CRAB

Cheering ruptured
A clearing sky
With fresh wind raving
Royalty
Stood up to wave
A man with crown and beard to last
Much longer than his body arched

This king was really far too old
His dead voice no reverberation
So the bard spoke in his stead
Whilst the simple deaf king trusted
Without ever really knowing
What his people truly said

We thank these youths
Who think the truth is what they hear
So I decree they'll do their bit
Release our fairest
Sit in chains
Until our promise has been met
To feed the beast
And keep our king
Alive with us
For then the golden laser might
Last for yet another year

Astra and Sebastian

Stuck squatting together inseparable
Were chained so tight they couldn't sit
Sebastian and Astra gripped
Each other's hand as their maid ran
Euphorically
To watch in safety up the cliff

Just at that moment breaking water
Rapids eddies salty torture
Rose a spectacle more apt
To stagnate a beating heart
And yet how this strange crowd clapped

Through all the noise
Our heroes saw
A massive crab
With larger claws
And armour plated
Saucer eyes
Arise to dominate the water

This massive beast of orange shell
Dimensions that the claws would fell
A china wall created yells
A permanantly screaming yelp
For help that echoes
Round the walls of cavern caves
To chill the heart of hot young braves

It ripped their chains
And for a moment
Thought them saved
But swallowed whole
And in one breath

Astra and Sebastian

The beast she lurched and dived for brine
For endless underwater time

Now sliding down a sodden gullet
They landed bump inside its stomach
A vast low hall of glowing spindles
Water stilled first made the flesh
Have sensual tingles but then burnt
As acid mingled to digest

They scrambled up her sloping bowl
Clinging to the wobbly wall
But not so easy not to fall
In time they slipped then gripped again
Crazed splitting legs from skidding feet
That couldn't find a grip

He bounced his fist off fleshy walls
Whilst Astra smartly donned her hood
And dove as deeply as she could
Through darkness swam a hole she found
Round dark intesines down and out
Into the ocean flouting death

He saw her go but fewer clothes
To copy her escape and so
Sebastian grew braver mad
Perhaps a mixture of them both

He scrambled through her stomach
Gullet
To her throat
The acid splashing
Up his legs

Astra and Sebastian

Clawed
Creeping crept
His sore eyes weeping
Onion tears
Into her jaw
His only thought
Was quickly formed
I've got to get the hell from here

Inside her mouth
He bent and pushed
To brace himself on her palate
With new found strength
Opened her jaw
Although she clamped and bounced back down
He pushed on more
And quickly found
The sight of light and water rushing
Washing him provided more
He thrust a final throw and surely
Dived to freedom through her maw

Enraged and hurt
Her meal escaped
She smote her claws
Onto the ocean
Aiming for Sebastian
Who'd gone elsewhere
Avoiding scare
Had swum around to her blind side
Dashing one eye in with his foot

Blind on one side
The right one wrong

Astra and Sebastian

She span around in circles long
For no real reason other than that
She had lost the will to plan

Sebastian swam for the coast
But soon her lonely vision
Caught him
Roared and charged
Crossing the waves
With angers forced speed
Closed the gap

A few more seconds panted out
Into those longer minutes more
Whilst all the eyes upon the shore
Envisioning the pure disaster
Where their gift might have refused
To give as much as they were used to

Within this tragic maudlin moment
The king stepped off his throne and aged
Much faster than those watching stood
Could ever really have thought he could

From witnessing his test of time
The desperate trade of sacrifice
Explode into the myth it was
He staggered slowly to the end

The pier like him required repair
Retired himself with gallant words
His last remaining strength the birds
Heard older tones and breathed relief
That time would run not stand repeated

Astra and Sebastian

Stock still on its mill

My people friends and nobility
Please let my daughter lead you now
Rejuvenate our bolder city
Stagant in soliloquoy
From trading life for length
My candle burnt out moons ago
Spluttered on by sacrifice
Through sending maidens to a fate
That still awaits my final roll
The crab who won me paradise
Asked for my boxed soul as a price
If life had been magnificent
Once seven years of reign had passed
Look at my broken body worn
And desolate their dead hands haunt me
Who would want me any more
I'm not a king just a decree
Who's lingered on O woe is me
Not forty years but forty days
Is how a man or king is made
For what we've traded just for more
Is cancerous and fraught of care
An unbecoming growth of mouth
You shouldn't whisper boys just shout
To keep your world of joys alive
For all must pass a burning sun
Would make us cinders if not set
In rythym with the other boon
The softer tranquil moonlit night
For it's no good turning to staid
The pleasure which at first engaged
So if your smile is used to wish

For future wealth not sure release
From all the helplessness of trials
Go gently slide into the typhoon
And take it now don't wait regret
To hold on hard with cracking nails
For compensation from a past
You never let yourself engage
Weep first for surely you will cry soon
Leap at will or tides they'll push you
Now goodbye for I must ride
Into the setting sun of debt
They've kept on hold for me

The king collapsed into a heap
Of purple robes
Rolled off the pier into the claws
Of our poor crab who finally
Could get what she's entitled to

His guards rushed to defend the sword
But honour given to the globe
The fragile earth had been repaid
Replaced as head of nature's table
Guiding urges toasting all
The king is dead long live the queen
And so by voice was order too
Quite easily restored

18. DRIFT

The water caught in his throat coming up
For rising too fast with a tremulous gulp
Strove hard to be heard over the fury and gulls

Astra and Sebastian

O Astra where are you
Astra where are you

From somewhere down deeper than Davy's old locker
Came an unconscious feeling surfing fast on the ether
A purer light than illumination
A sickness much richer and full of explosion
Than past petty violence
Or crystalised salt in the stomach

On top of the sea Sebastian
Was splashing Astra
For though they surfaced far apart
Were brought together by the art
Of currents and a story's heart
Each spitting water platitudes
Of timeless wonder at the other
If only they could hear themselves
If only they could hear each other

Whilst off the waves the evening sparkle
Of the sun played with them too
A childish game
But now their eyes were knowing darker
Astra splashed back
Felt him stronger
Dived and plunged
Allowing skin to linger on for
Neither fain to know the end
Born heralding this new adventure
The simple life that's eaten plain
Until the climax of the game
Can finally be savoured

Astra and Sebastian

The silver moon replaced the sun
Attracted to their magic whirl
They almost lifted clean the water
As that which knows its edge is done
All life is held within this moment
Sebastian and Astra kissed
And thus forever had begun

After the meeting comes the rest
They floated in each other's arms
To watch a golden haze rise up
Over off the wedding veil
Revealed the cliffs
A mist unmissed
Shed from this town lost to a wish

The folks on the quay were finally seeing
Each other as human and finding the key
And singing new rhymes of two fabulous children
Creating a future through mythology

Twirling in the blue blue water
Tumultuous tides and swirling currents
Carry them far from old objects of strife
Whilst a bold harvest moon sparks fresh off the brine
Opulent laughter lists on the breeze

Beckoning darkness drew colours to grey
As light finally led its euphoria to bed
For nothing to see when you know of your way
As the wild worldly noise is the blanket of muses
That keeps temples throbbing and hearts stoutly pounding
So too our new heroes have seen how to live

Astra and Sebastian

The night wearing on can halt all perception
When once moving laughter goes static and drowns
Now flocking brash seabirds swoop curling and diving
Each mocking our lovers you can't hope to drop
Or pass o'er an edge that you'd rather hold up
With unstable gasses you won't even try
The limit is set and what's more it's certain
You definitely cannot yet fly

You hear them asked Sebastian
So many ears have lived their loss
She laughingly replied with spray in her eyes
The salt teasing hair into weeds

O let us keep spinning the church is macabre
Your arms on my back and mine round your waist
Will form us a ball to traverse all the waves
A galleon so gallant with rakish delight
A merkaba to play in where we can be safe
On a dazzling aura of light

So let us return some of that which is lost
And spin off the edge to challenge the sun
For he always comes back
Like the truth and the soul
And the cycles of nature rotating the soil
A waterfall of pleasure
Is not what I measure
For quite how we changed
In that petulent crab
I can't put my finger on
But you I can grab

Sebastian's silence was the greatest reply

Astra and Sebastian

As they span through the night
And then span through the day
Whilst jellyfish shoals and the lost dolphin's pawed
The bubbles of bladderwurt popping 'till dawn

Skimming like stones they passed the horizon
To witness another extended from there
With no questions asked any fool can float past
Serene as an answer that's given or shared

The mid distance forged an indelible point
With a gentle exhale the sun set behind them
They bumped for some sand formed the hem of the land
And the breakers washed over them clean

I'm hungry he grumbled
His stomach the pertinent organ of speech
I'm lonely she mocked
Put your arms back and greet
This heart with your heart
Only then shall we eat

Sat late on the sand with a fire and the stars
Entwined with the changes of flickering flames
The quartz round the hearth had sparkled like glass
Till gentle breeze blew the long evening to dreams

You're tired I'm alive
She contined to whisper
Let's turn today's embers
Back into hot flame

As they rolled in the sand
The breeze off the ocean

Astra and Sebastian

Became quite a gale
Which bent all the palm trees
Whose leaves whipped as light rain
Washed salt and the fun from their minds

The creepers were creeping
And monuments shifting
The air seems alive with a challenge
I feel it
And whilst it's not cold
If this rain gets much stronger
We'll definitely have to be swift

The wet wood it crackled
Weird mystery metaphor
Caught up in surprise
As time was suspended
In a blink of their eyes

Heavy clouds broke with an unblessèd rain
As forked lightening struck on the hill
The hill that rose steep from the beach and was still
Now thrashed around wildly all covered in forest
And shadows that threatened to kill
When thunder chased hot on the tail of lightning
They no longer knew what was real

Crouched deep like a sunset
Where the sand met the forest
A tree had been struck
Forcing fire to flare brightly
Alive as the day

Then behind all the flames

A silent and frighening
Hulking slunk silhouette
Crept out towards them
To help with the trembling
They both held their breath

19. LION TRIAL

A gargantuan lion
He proud as he prowled
His mane came alive
In the flames of the fire

The jungle a palette
This lion its muse
Iconic intrinsic
Artistic in view

With golden eyes fixed them
Stung Astra Sebastian
Exposed on the beach
Now marked in the dark

The forest no master
Yet fast the leaves parted
And wilted the grasses
On hearing his ominous roar

The lovers so startled
They fell to the floor

For nothing's as stark
As a comment you store

Astra and Sebastian

Try brushing off wet sand
And trying to balance
As scenery changes
Beyond your command

For waiting behind
The wilting bent trees
Was a circle of stones
And behind all of those
A temple reposed

Serene ghostly stable
The stones felt much older
Than the colours diffused
By the petulant storm

But its majesty vanished
Like the traces of time
Its carved façade fading
As the lion magnificent
Prowled out of its shadows
To stand on the sand

His flashing eyes bright
Took the flames out the fire
The reticent embers
Collapsed for respite

Arching his back
And flashing his iris
His golden tail stroking
The sky in delight
A clever cat tactic
To question your own prey

Astra and Sebastian

Like the constellation riding the night

The lion's broad shoulders
Sensed victory bolder
A massive vibration
He bellowed again
Which buried his quarry
In raptures of ignorance
Unable to think for themselves

Just then came the charge
The lion loomed larger
Sand flying back from his on-rushing paws

Quartz span in the rain
Reflecting the stars
All covered by clouds
And the day
Lost to nothing
A fashionable cause
No cause for delay

Our humans stood lonely
Still standing their ground
When Sebastian boldly
Grabbed onto her hand

Rending their senses
The moment had gone
Completing the hardest task
Of making step one

Their feet beat a drum
On the solid wet sand

Astra and Sebastian

Like the veins now pulsating
The side of their head

So long was the sand
They ran to the tide
Where sharp water broken
Whipped through like a scythe

Chopping their ankles
The storm had aroused it
Dragging them deeper
Like emotive secrets
They tripped
And were thrown
Down onto the sand
In perfect submission
But without command

She grabbed in the panic
Imploring him up
Have patience
My love
Stand your ground
And your glove
For there's nothing between
A hard slap in the face
Or death and the sound
Of a silent because

The sand and the sand
With the lion still pounding
Sebastian shouted
Pushing Astra to safety
Distracting the lion

Astra and Sebastian

The beach and the planned
For the distance
Is narrowing
A trance
And the lion
Is closer
A hair's breadth
The edge of its mane
The warmth of its breath
One flash of its eyes
Was a struggle in silence
Sebastian inside
Turned to jelly
Denied
All the instincts
His belly
Forsaken
The claws
On the paws
Of the lion
Poised to strike
Down upon him
The fleeting
Retreating
Dilating bold iris
Of a boy
Made a man
By the laws of the chase
Sebastian rose
To the challenge
Imploded
By quenching old fears
In a moment
Was born

Astra and Sebastian

Not one pause for thought
Rolled aside
From the stare
Violent jaws snapped on air
As the lion flew on past

Progression is muted
For the lion had to pass through
The infinite point of a turn

This one brittle moment
Was frozen inside of the tropical storm
So when he had turned
Faced the man on the ground
There's a change in the battle
For the humans have recourse to plan

The horn from his back
Has rolled in the struggle
Away 'cross the black sand
He saw it and suddenly
Knew just what to do

Please help me he cried
Blow for help on the horn
So Astra was dashing
Through the slicing harsh rain
Far over the dark sand
Till the horn was a rose
At her lips and was blown
To the corners of earth
With a supple strong long lowly sound

Before the proud storm

Astra and Sebastian

Lowed this subtlest tone
With the clearest success
Over that which is known

For in but a short breath
The beach was embraced
By an army of ghosts
Superlative faces
Stood facing the rain

Each living and well
They solidified time
As the people stood still
With the stones of the temple
All calling for home

The power was stored
And the army charged up
Now they surged into battle
With the Ram at their front

Just one horn but proud
His hard head rushed down
Fervent flesh legs as metal
Braced handsomely for the next round

Meeting the lion at the peak of return
Hot fire sought its flame
In a thunder clap mountain
The water front lapped
Finally Astra shouted
Sebastian throated
A guttural cry

Then the air was all still
Letting time to catch up
Like the blood dying red
Of the lion lying dead on the sand

The mythical creatures evaporated
Our heroes embraced
At the end of the battle
The making of state
From the vision of mind

The flowering of identity
Is believing the certainty inside of self
Openly letting another in
No shame in asking for help

20. AN ELEMENTAL TEMPLE

Awake from the stupor
Of blood sweat and tears
The Ram off to wait for
Return of his horn

Turned from the sea
They looked at the stone
Which held transcendental
Thoughts elemental
Old meaning in known
New symbols revealed

The natural explosion of sensitive roses
To intrusion of light in the morning supposes
Experience that's known and conducive to time

Astra and Sebastian

Like the fall of the throne
Or the sun making dew for the grass

The ornate crafted entrance
Of the timeless temple
Now tempted them both from
The bold unpredicatable
Struggle of life

Safely preserved from unscrupulous calls
The walls didn't threaten but beckoned them in
So towards them they walked
Without feeling rushed or the push of the breeze
Or a sense of intrusion or call

Up steps that would mark the start of their journey
Together they floated
On past the twinned chimera
That guarded this primal doorway

Like lions they'd fought
And finished for all
Traversing this threshold
To the node of the temple
Could hold nothing new
To two hearts who've made
This journey before
Escaping the bowels of the crab of the soul
And the cancerous doubt it can hold

Past blazing lit torches
A fire at its gate
The palace held ash
Which mottled in chinks of their light

Astra and Sebastian

Probing on deeper
Were suddenly shrouded
By all of these chimneys
Of enlightened dust
Which caught in their noses
Whilst sneezing wide echoed
Moved into this passage of night

Acoustically designed
Then cardinally aligned
Along an old axis
Framed long in the past
Designed by the earth
And so built to last

They walked slowly through many vast column halls
Each piled high with treasure
Large casks cast in gold
Each etched with the life lines
The wisdom of old

Touching the wall
Of the farthest hall
They opened a door
And saw a dark passage
Its low floor retreating
To triangle focus

A cavernous maze to the uninitiated
Riddled with tunnels they permeated
Stone but our adventurers
Were drawn along the path they'd chosen
A labyrinth of least resistance
As the Ram had wished of them

Astra and Sebastian

For freedom won is simply knowing
That first you must
Talk with the one
Who watches guards
The gates of thought
To help those learnèd
Not to think to harm their kind
By exploitation of the mind

O Astra Sebastian
Of a thousand leagues
Of hidden stars
Unfathomable depths
O come my Astra Sebastian pass

Across the passageway a wall
Yet from its middle through a door
Shone bounteous light that warmly beckoned
Shadowed them and held in thrall
The cold silhouette of uncountable beasts
The horrible edge of the eager self
Was challenged dropped then left behind

O Astra Sebastian
From the crown of your head
To the base of your heart
Relieve yourselves of one item part
With some possession in deference to pass

At every gate further
Till seven were passed
Was offered this chant
And one piece of clothing
Was discharged from duty

Astra and Sebastian

And left in the path

Sebastian however kept hold of the horn
For his was to guard not to own and discard

On passing each gate so the light changed to dark
And then back to light when they passed the next gate
Until they reached heaven the heart and eighth chamber
All bathed in a glow now surrounding the dark path
Whilst those in the dark would have just seen a pathway
And lunge for the old temple's gold
Missing the beauty and wisdom about

For on the high walls were the paintings of ancients
Sayings and patterns of moveable stars

Now faded to sandstone
But anticipating
The next timely passenger
Passing through here

We mustn't forget that the colour was there
Their faces in profile pointing the way

So naked they stood
Preserving the centre
In front of an altar
Upon which was stood
A set of paired statues
Two beautiful women
As twins one was lovely
The other one cursed
Where one held a smile
The other reverse

Astra and Sebastian

The first one as flesh
She cradled an egg
The other was bones
Her hands clutched a stone
Raised high up and waiting
To smash on the egg

Resplendent in jewels
The colours span spectral
In wide spiral light
A braclet snake necklace
The left wrist was glowing
An anklet the right foot
Tied them to the earth
Had golden ringed toes
One each for the seasons
And one for the close
As icons at large
These statues remarkable
Inspired thoughts inside them
With joy and its worth

Linking lone minds
With the horror of arms
And the heart of the humans who
Though born with soil
To opposites sustinence
And subjective toil
Are finally sure
Of the infinite all
And feel a reunion
That carries their future
Along with the stars

Astra and Sebastian

Welcome please Astra
Sebastian Welcome
Now here you are near the whole centre of you
The nadir where your souls are reborn or untrue

Welcome please Astra
Sebastian welcome
You're pure in your knowledge and pure in your heart
Let infinite future meet infinite past

And with the blazing light of
A million suns behind them
Those powerful flares
That don't hunger for fuel
They saw through their dark
Silhouettes as clear glass
Transparent and lucid
With the sand gleaming golden beneath

Releasing both slowly the wisp of a breath
Like a midsummer's wind
Gently blowing the mist
From that mystical cliff top
They emptied themselves
And their souls joined the rest

Wiping the tears
They flexed all their aching cold muscles as new
And reached with their hands
For the gentlest strength
An emergency service
To rescue yourself

As one felt the other

Another the same
Their uncoiling soul
Curled into its opposite
The natural goal
Of a wonderful game
This wealth of desire
Giving senses a hand
Made love with their all
Got all covered in sand

21. RISING UP AND AWAY

The explosion expanded
The connection was made
The tunnels of life now an infinite page
The sanctum receded
The inner the outer
The shell and the nut
Sebastian and Astra
Flew up to the heavens
To sit on each side
Of the cosmic scales balanced
Pure dishes of light

The blind eye of Sirius
Saw them there and blinked
Whilst Polaris stopped thinking
And joined with the dragon
Draped long round her sleeve

The Pliades moved
As they watched over Pisces
Together forever as one at once all

Astra and Sebastian

The cosmos revealed
Through its paramount cycle
Constellations hailed them
Orion was pleased
Held out to them both
His warrior's sword
Accepted to brotherhood
Are those who have grown
To address the same trials
That gave him his home

The father has mercy
All guilt is misplaced
The new generation
The parents replaced
His hand on their shoulders
A mighty decree
Command all your lands
As a universe seen

Sebastian offered the breast plate of war
As king of the cosmos a blunted sword
Whilst Astra enrobed in the white of the pure
A halo of thorns made queen of the lore

The strings of the scales
Shortened up to the fulcrum
A moveable one
Now binding together
The centre invisible
The equity of difference
Is equality

They saw all the colours

Astra and Sebastian

Its opulent spectrum
The darkness between
Each galaxy spinning
Around a translucent
Fresh hurricane wind

Then down to a stream
In a forest where children
Make ripples with rocks
On a pool that could look
Like a whole solar system
Its placid face shimmered
Like the sky in a dream
Reflecting your plot
And perhaps what it means

Dove smoothly beneath
To the atoms within
Spun seamlessly round
Going deeper and then
When the nucleus beats
Found nothing again

So just like the scales
They fell through it all
To the land of bold plans
And young humans whilst knowing
The beginning is token
The end for a fool
Who thinks logic's something
Without an assumption
A stool to sit on
Its heel of Achilles
Exposed for us all

Astra and Sebastian

Harmonious rhythm unpeeled itself
From behind the lost space of invisible shade
Eternity's timeless tumultuous wave
The tiniest lances of time's lot emerged
The greatest vibration of circumstance
Where inspectors tremble
The comfortable dance

When caught in the trance
Of pure fabulous lore
Absolute Understanding
Means Silence
And more

So nothing was spoken
As the cosmotic mother
And brother together
Wired into a tone
Gave faces to every pure cycle of form
From the smallest electrons
To the beautiful all

Gold emanations of the unspoken word
At the invisible fulcrum that steadies us all
The wobble 'till life is infinitely still
And dead to the fall or the will to be spun

Sublime as a moment
No longer in time
Where shakti chi energy
Puts a name to the skill

A peace when the balance
Is suddenly real

And nothing means everything
Comparison nil

All noise is still
The truth unemcumbered
By reasonable steering
Or soulless demands of the will

Pass gentle through zero
As you pass through a wall
When the gate is left open
To those who will walk

22. THE LAND OF NE'ER DESTROYED

Together Sebastian and Astra awoke
Their ears flowering open
To the humming of air
Although neither spoke
She gently moaned once
At the touch of her love on her hair

Awaking salt taste
On the tip of the tongue
Lost memories of smell
When the nose was still young

Their eyelids a flutter
The beach into focus
The sand lying gold
By a sapphire blue sea

Deliciously stretching their toes and rolled over

Astra and Sebastian

The morning was fetching a glance at each other
The ocean the trees the horizon mid air
To the end of the sky brightly blue and still bare
Initially yawning as if new life was dawning
The savouring prospect of truth maybe more then
Reflect on before and what has passed though unaware

The temple had fallen
All its walls now surmounted
By mosses and trees
Brave roots curling lost stones
New form to debris
From aquamarine flesh
To green natural mortar
Each reclaimed the structure
Made circles from squares

The walls have all fallen
Sebastian pointed
She murmured it's beautiful
What more could we hope for
When nature she shapes
She draws out the purest
Forms from the water
Let's drink at her brook
Take a look whilst we're there
For I think we've arrived

Sebastian cried
I know we've arrived
From the void to a substance
This breath of abundance
Is the place that was promised
All senses employed

Astra and Sebastian

This must be the Land of Ne'er Destroyed

They pushed past the ruins and on through the foliage
That gave all the vista a tearful uniqueness
A coming of age when you feel a completeness
A fondness for detail and expectance to share

For each vibrant bird whistling messages of love
A patter of hooves drifts behind every tree
Past soft babbling brooks more gentle than silence
As nothing is said when so nice to agree

Their footprints remained in the soft mossy turf
A trace of their pathway from never to there
Beyond all the foliage a mountain before them
With concentric spirals of streets up and down
A town made of towers sticking out of the hill
A flowering landscape of storeys in wood

Each tower was tussling as if multiplying
Near massive vast statues of morphed personality
Their face to the clouds as our heroes ran forwards
To be in amongst it to live in this land

Some books with their leaves spread
Flew off from tall piles
That all teetered upwards
Flamboyant and red

Each offered their spell to the transient light
Words trickled like feathers
As clouds separated
To leave the sky bright

Astra and Sebastian

Curled out through the thermals
Around the capped peak
Was a cobweb like mist
Of sparkling connection

Light rode on grey horses
Along these deft pathways
The silk was supplied
By the massive white spider
Spinning in the sky

The sun caught behind her
A perfect round circle
The mount intersected
For tangents important
When changing dimension
The mountain's alive so Sebastian said

Soon found they were winding
Up a tudor housed street
The upper floors leering
Each stretching and leaning
Blocking the sky
With the lives of more people
The black and white stressed wood
Of history complete

Touched heads at the top floor
It unified lots
Or the sides seen as separate
We know as a street

Sebastian spoke to the craning necks
That peered and cheered from crowded windows

Astra and Sebastian

Whilst Astra read the doorbell lists
The thirsty pages of history
Of those no longer missed

A ground floor bell read Arkhenaten
The first floor Adam
Many others
Jesus Christ
Muhammad living on the third
And like those in proximity
Each shouting for identity
Inside the house of just one God

Hand in hand they ran away
Up this uncoiling spiral street
Still ringing loud
Wherever found
Uncountable doorbells
The shouting inside
Amused them but hearing
Lone fragments of time
Inspired in their minds
A place to go back to
A spark for a fire

They pushed through descending
Mass protests flag wavers
The pagans and pacifists
Forced out of their homes

Burst into a clearing
A library of huge stones
Pythagorus peering
Whilst furiously scribbling

Astra and Sebastian

From carvings and tomes
Then putting his name like many before him
To something he found not something he'd made

At the peak of the climb here a pillar reclined
A yardstick formation from astral design
Or a powerful calender built upwards in stone
Where the sun and the stars mark the passage of time
Temples some smiling then crying in stages
As priests touch somebody
With wisdom or favours

Now on down the far side
Of the concentric spiral
Away in the distance
The pyramids stand
All grassy with age
The step and the grand
One raised up for power
And one for the ages
Another to death
When they misread the pages
But none for the dead
Who are buried by sages

The book of the infinite lessons of language
Where concepts are names in a translation's shell
Old reified dreams put away into pasture
A costume remains when the body has melted
For fences and hedges will rot into dust
When the concept's inside them
Like the constantly growing long grasses have not

Then later came marbles and statues of men

Astra and Sebastian

A citidel standing alone in a hell
Was cleared of all forest it groaned with the smell
Of bearing a truth it now wished it forgot

The black house of pillage
The feminine parlour
From the cellar of sellers to the towers of opinion
Where candles drip hot in the attics of artists
Like nudists aware of the power inside
When you bare all to people to share in your life

The warmest of kitchens with diligence of trade
To ignorant bedrooms where birds in their cages
Dream of redemption or windows left open
Whilst those eating quail's eggs are lonely and scared
Of boys in the parlour caught munching leftovers
Despondent from serving make takeover plans

The raising of power carried them fast down the hill
And on to long valleys where worms eat their fill
Of the remnants of ages that learnt only killing
Forgetting what built them forgoing their skills

Down here and there a wanderering ghost
Would cross their path some permanently blind
Passed through their bodies and on to more forest
Except for a few glowing magi who waited
With a wave of encouragement
These riding along on the cycles of knowledge
No rings of entrapment weighing heavy their hands
Their warm friendly faces clad simply in robes
Where others wore silk
Which caught on the branches
And made them exposed

Astra and Sebastian

Our heroes saw all on their walk through the infinitely
Long squirming legs of the octopus of knowledge
Whose eternal tentacles get parried by life
From the struggle of hand before mind over monsters
To muddled modernity pushed out to its cliff
An absolute limit that no one has built
The truths underlying the views of the relic
The values of later placed onto the past
The parting of mists made the walk psychedelic
At once empathetic but able to grasp

Felt love for it all for the fire for the strife
For themselves for the laughs and the cooking for life
For the jury the poorly still captured in stone
Or metal worked purely for the forging of skill
And the pleasure of bettering your own stubborn will

23. A FLOATING ISLAND

History repeating they walked until dawn
When frost was retreating away from the lawn
The clearest of nights paradoxically was warmed
By staring at stars running soil through their fingers
Not feeding a bonfire or staving a yawn

Till come on the morn climbing over a rock
Were the guests of a scorpion flat on his back
Grinning at nothing and sunning himself
For knowing he fears only that which he hasn't seen
They heard its soft whisper there's much more to come
Keep watching for signs my curious ones

Its tail pointed east

Astra and Sebastian

So now onwards and on
Till the vista exploded
Bejewelled with the morning
A placid lake finished
By an ornate pagoda
And lain out inside
Was a generous breakfast
Hot on the table
Long benches for more
Than our weary heroes
For others will surely join in the fable

Whilst watching the water
They saw as they munched
A reclining island
Of feminine shape
That span with a turn of
Twenty four minutes
Enough for four courses
Six minutes apiece
Some hot bread then veg
With a drink and a breath

Uncommon in lapping
Fresh wash of the breeze
Rotated this Goddess
Lying calm radiating
Inexorable beauty

Floating in the mist
Of peace and tranquility
She slept like the cast
Of a fairy tale woven
Together and into

Astra and Sebastian

Its own simple spell

A boat lay precisely where it ought in these moments
And taking an oar each
Drew fast from the shore
A wind of enchantment
The lake hardly moved

Whisking through water not once wishing more
They sailed like a soft cloud not tainting the air
There soon came a bump and tying the painter
Stepped off their small boat to tread on the shore

Then scrambled atop this majestic nude vision
Whose dark skin was glowing accustomed to charm
A face born of mercy closed eyes and warm lips
She slept half submerged with her power beneath

They crept past her shoulder through tresses of dreadlocks
And calm open ears where her body began
All tattooed with whys and the wherefores of life
Magnificent marks to the beauty of dust
A tale of the planets she watched as she dreamed of
Breathing together impossible dreams
The sowing of seeds for the just

They stared at her face for could hardly pull out
Of its grace walking backwards across
Her ripe breasts heaving laden with breath
And swollen with journeys the milk for the quest

Turned on her stomach to now face her feet
They saw a tall tree with its vast twisting branches
Holding many broad leaves

Astra and Sebastian

Its trunk was drunk leaning
Away at an angle twenty three degrees
And wobbling around as if going to sea

And so as she span through the changing of days
She watched the sun move through twelve ages of twelve

By its roots was her navel a deep well of sound
Around which the world seemed to spin in its round
When the Norse tell of Yggdrasil not exaggeration
To tell you each culture builds their myths on this

Sebastian reached round for the horn from his back
As Astra in rapture was starting to sway
Whilst humming a tune that owed all its depth to
The sound sweetly floating from inside the source

A chord tale that thrummed and vibrated for ever
From inside the vortex
And into the cortex
Sung with each other a powerful spell

He dipped in the horn and filled it with water
But felt not to drink for the wisdom was in him
Ghosts whispered death is a blessing let thought in
Imagination story stay strong through the pain
And elation of life not eternities plain

Then raising the horn from the softest skin
The sky shattered cracked into bolts of fresh lightning
With thunder its heels how it rained with the joy
Broke summers hot boredom wild dancing in fields

24. A MAGICAL FLIGHT

Our heroes rose with it
Danced proud where they stood
Upon her soft stomach warm rising and falling
The mother she shuddered
Lips cracking to smile
Rolled onto her side
With a mumble and mutter
Of love and the other
Rose up from the lake
Now floating on air
Still spinning around

Now Astra and Sebastian
Thrown by this convulsion
Sailed out through the hot air
Lost not with confusion
Or panic reclined
On their back
Soaring glided
Allowing the air
To gently placate them
And cradle their form

Their bodies rushed down
With cosmic attraction
The water gushed up
To touch then engulf them
But here was the earth
And their collective trust
Running beside them
Super consciousness

Astra and Sebastian

For through a crack in the tumultuous sky
There came a flaming arrow bright
Long flat and wide it scooped them up
And gently bore them out of sight

Flown faster forth than light of day
A pathway coursed through wider heaven
Star baths shimmered
Comet's tails of ice were lifting
Clouds and sands of quartz aloft
Graceful in the softest rush
Of life called back to what it's lost

A crack of light
Blurred colour
Spectrums
All as one
And all at once
For who can tell without
A measure
Or the life of
Repetition

Its journey done the arrow banked
And dropped them into softest grass
One final barrel roll it lasted
Brushing earth for just a moment

Before ascending in a flash
Back to its realm inside the slowest
Lines of lives and objects floating
Into chaos out of time

The fresh wrinkles of innocence

Astra and Sebastian

Or bold the folds of agèd wisdom
Beginning does become the end
Two sides of paper share a page

From in the horn held by his hand
One single drop it fell to earth
A flower sprang to taste the sky
Charming land beyond a why

They laughed with water wet the dew
For all the snow from mountains melting
All the petals radiated
And as they laughed shook dry with mirth

The phoenix girl
And dragon boy
Gargantuan lion
The chorus line
A pantheon
As then the trickster
And the crab
Took their applause
And bowed before
The audience
Soon adding sound
With their own paws
Acknowledging the technical crew
Before making an aisle
To let the Ram step forth and smile

A grand welcome
To both my darlings
Your prayer has flowered
Like precious birth

Astra and Sebastian

My daughter earth
Empowered star
My son of time
Enamoured path
Sublime the signs
You've shown are clear
And valuable within your lives
The water and the force of trust
Does generate fresh air

Our pair reflected the glow of these thoughts
Caught in the flow of a glorious feeling
The hopes and fear of your soul's dominion
Freed to walk with nature's bidding
Now was the time for Sebastian to offer
Ceremoniously the horn
Up to the Ram who knelt before him
Immediately it touched the nub
They fused together
As if the world was never apart
The life giving water
Doing its job

Inevitably here all the spirit was spilt
So distraught Sebastian
Almost cold disappointed
Spoke out before thinking
Don't waste all the water
For which we have fought
We've travelled too long for the magic to wane

The magic is here
Has already been done
The ram wisely smiled

Astra and Sebastian

You've already begun

And then he decreed
You've no need for water
Or things you can lose
Your world needs no offerings
I'll wait here for you
And for any other
That like you will choose
To go on the quest to renew our existence
Make our flesh as strong
And our fur like our eyes
Full bright and alive
So they see us like you do
And they know they've arrived

Sebastian's eyes welled tearful with pride
As he stood certain on his ground
And earthly ceremony found
A medallion pinned
Upon his vital chest
Felt the cosmos spin
The silent grin
With everything he'd the pleasure to know
And now knew how to show

25. THE RETURN

As Astra and Sebastian bowed
The golden Ram stood up and ploughed
A final furrow to the ground
Three symbiotic satellites
All waltzing in a flurry cloud

Astra and Sebastian

I'll call the sage to take you back
You children of the corn and match

A centaur stepped out from the crowd
Of loud once exiled faces proud
The very beasts of magic's figment
Filaments of permanence
Historical
Hysterical
Realities made
From comical images
How we can imagine life

An ancient intricate style of building
The wielding of theoretical tools
A keystone to all types of arches
Mortar to the mason's rules
Now drawn upon this beast man walking
Simply plain and illustrating
Every connection in us all

Come walk with me
His rare voice boomed
I'll show you fields
Where horizons loom
And dreams are woven into fact
Warm citadels to house the droves
Of children no more left alone
I'll never thank you enough for that
But can show you to home

Wow what a time
It's hard to go
Sebastian whispered just to Astra

Astra and Sebastian

I know she smiled
And held his hand

We'll never really leave this place
Let us maintain it in the names
We give to that we know as fact
To understand distant translations
Where language has forgotten that
We'll be redrawn in other places
Precious to our heart these faces
Interpolate like dreams need spaces
A notion for the coming verse
A meditation every motion
Mantra as our speech rehearsed
Attached to cycles from our own
The blood that flows
To those that grow around us blow
A wind in which true seeds will grow
Surround us till the universe
Can integrate with what we do
We've seen its form as people too
So treat them with a due and lo
We soon can choose what's understood
Know too that nothing truly exists
As objects crumble into dust
Allow the thought to receive its just
Reward and disappointment falls
We're now sharing the infinite all
A ring is more than a metal band
A bond to glitter in your mind
Formidable evil eternal good
The colours are a spectrum thrown
About the people repetition
Solidified by mystic forms

Astra and Sebastian

Include desires
And fan the flames
Let action work these paeans out
A selfish act or altruism
Will bubble cauldrons of debate
To challenge each and every form
And through the rush will people form
A shared opinion gentle born
A hero's fall to check it works
And icons sure to halt the dirge
Of time that changes forms of life
Into a world we can see right
For hate breeds worse
Regurgitates its lowly form
So too will hope and all that's fine
To reason us with greater rime
Give all youself to love don't try
To hold it as your own for worse
Will bitter berries grow and drip
Their sour felt juice from on your lips
Just do for time and add to this
Rich tapestry no paradox
For anything that's tried and tested
Will be agreed by others jested
Argued worked and manifested
From on the dot of form to where
Our history tells the tale of wary
Souls who crave an art or place
Creating our reality
Now smoothly draw the arrow back
And vibrate coupled with release
The dynamite of supple strength
Infinity's first tangible
Fine line beyond eternal hearts

And all between
That we're a part of
Cycles forming constructs spinning
See a sister
Brother father mother blissful
Know them as we know those more
For you will love like I love you
And when I know you love me too

Her voice brought peace to the listening deer
Who promised all to stay the same
Though time decrees you'll always change

As now they'd come to their return
That place they started in despair
Beside the pool
A flowered grove
The centaur reared
Said thank you dears
And disappeared into the dawn

26. A NEW AGE

A misty wistful effluvia
Hung longing from their heavy shoulders
As in hand the timely lovers
Astra and Sebastian
Made slow their walk back to their home

Throughout the forest under brush
And over rivers
Passed once charred and blackened roots
Bracken green and holly red

Astra and Sebastian

The mistletoe bright white and fresh
For winter was in deepest thrall
Solstice marked not long ago
And though no snow was very cold
Their breath a mist upon the face

Sebastian said can't wait to show you
All my old haunts and secret places
Take you to the market castle
Show you faces tell you stories
Introduce you to my home

But such a shock awaited both
As first a noise like blackened butter
Then some concrete asphalt tougher
Although they'd not yet met such matter
Climbed up banks of greying grass
To see a thousand cars rush past

And though they'd passed through danger's pleasure
Fought the beasts of will's dilemma
Saw infinity as settled
Nothing could've prepared them for
This mask upon reality

Stood open jawed the restless morn
Where all these objects flung together
Hot lights burnt the lowest branches
Towards horizon's yawning dawn

Towers scraped the sky the birds
Were wheeling round this angled jaw
And Astra's eyes told more than words
Shock oozing from her every pore

Astra and Sebastian

More from a curiousness than force
They followed like an elder pilgrim
The curving road with double yellow
Lines to guide solemn procession

Eyes were raised up to the heavens
As the streets contracted in
The shops they only recognized
By some old wares that still had use
But all electrical or plenty
Was a sight bewildering

How long away Sebastian stuttered
Was but a week or maybe more
A year at most counting the moon
But how the pages have been turned

They flew like arrows to the centre
Where a castle and its keep
Lay grey eroded time and battle
Stones and tourists in a heap

And here was where they too became
The focus of a widened eye
For still dressed in the finer robes
The stars had once bestowed on them

Asta wore her halo proud
Sebastian his sword glowed true
The cameras clicked and people moved them
Into poses they deemed fine

So tired and weary day had taken
More than they could think to give

Astra and Sebastian

A journey with a new proportion
Craved to rest but had to live

The late night grin wore sore at them
As those in fancy dress will know
The cheering laughter at a costume
But unlike those in fancy dresses
These truly were their only clothes

So hungry and despondent fading
This is our town I know I know
Sebastian argued to Astra
Who wasn't really listening

Accepted first and then bowled over
The sea of life tumultuous flow
A low flyover gave protection
To those with nowhere else to go

Then bounding down the modern scree
Of cans and paper came a tramp
Wiry beard had he and hats
Two scarves wrapped round his ancient ears
To keep from cold lit up a fire
Inside a flecked and rusty pitcher

Stamped the ground and snorted breath
As buoyant steam before the night
Chewed on his sleeve his bright eyes danced
Then gave them first a passing glance
Before begrudingly a smile

Hey you two long and sallow faces
Lost your way after the party

Astra and Sebastian

What's got your goat I'm here to help
Please warm your hands the winter's nasty
About as nice as people show

Why thank you friend
Astra was hearty
You are the first to ask our health
Not just if that we might or can

But now I ask
Replied the tramp
It's getting on
You'd best be getting back
To somewhere warmer
Than this ramp

Then Astra glanced into the sky
I somehow think an eon's passed
Whilst we've been walking outer time
Our house has disappeared so fast
It's all so strange but since you've come
Once more I see our time has come

The tramp he smiled
Immediately knew
He recognized these travellers few
Did ever come but rumours flew

Not much has changed miss
Give it time not just a dash
For you will see beneath the varnish
To the clod of nutrients
Those fairer wishes brought to life
By breathing touching people's kisses

Astra and Sebastian

Built up added picturesque
To make this town it's not the best
But certainly like all the rest
Whatever time you mean

He waved a gnarled
Clasped hooflike hand
Around their cares
Which helped them fade
Go see our Julia he suggested
She always cares for them like you

Where might we find this hopeful sight
Sebastians' eyes glowed in the night

The highest floor of yonder tower
I've heard them speak of you before
But tell you this for free me boy
You is the spit of she that looks
After you sacred souls

Astra smiled back graciously
Immediately we'll go to her
A thousand thanks for showing us
The deeper beauty of your town
Our abstract concepts of the path
Are difficult to see in strife
Which always changes what you know
Should never think that you've arrived
Will you be alright here alone

Don't fret for me miss I'll be fine
Please off you go now don't be frightened
Them's upstairs don't understand

Astra and Sebastian

If metal boxes cost them grand
The cold your soul is freezing in
Is always more than winter's hand
And never warmed by fires of men
I'll warm my hands you've warmed my heart
As yet another valuable friend
Who understands what we all are
Now get some food you both look starved

So off they went
Suppressing hopes
Of meeting truly in the flesh
Not only blood
But somewhere warm they're understood

Beside the flats they congregated
Waiting for the elevator
Saw the amber lights as fire
The trees embodied vibrant towers
Uniting both to breathe for sure
Upon the earth as stars once more

Soon were whisked up eighty floors
Towards the surest storey of heaven
Brick and mortar can develop
Here is where the door popped open
They found themselves a corridor
On their right an alphabet
Graffiti scrawled onto the wall

Upon their left a brighter picture
The whole of town illuminated
Music playing in the distance
Led them on towards a door

Astra and Sebastian

Where fragrant light spilt out a halo
And opened wide before they knocked

Stood there alive was Julia
Perhaps much older
But complete
Her face improved serenity
Had found her place
The sun to meet

Sebastian went white and cried
I never did desert your side

And nor did I
She softly smiled
It's quite all right
His mother hugged him
Drawing Astra to them too
I couldn't stop you both from going
Your journey is the only life
And more than I could give to you

Why hey there gorgeous what a dress
Sebastian you have done well
And though I know why you have on
Such boisterous robes of difference
Go chuck them in my wardrobe now
And grab when there some modern clothes

For in this new
You too Sebastian

In this new age
We've learnt the trick is

Astra and Sebastian

Change with time as nature does
Air all our views as everywhere
Are flat restrictions of the past
We're all unique
Let's chat about it
But life is really what we share
And give a real attachment to
Those things we can't see with our eyes
Or work for own or make believe

The door is open to our circle
My living room where we all sit
And delve into the lonely soul
Discuss the methods of protection
From all messages of gain
Empowerment of education
Encourage by always impressing
Importance onto everything
And how it's interweaved

We give our changing congregation
A safe and steady place to go
Some music food with charm or magic
Of a friend finding your mood
Mythologies that understand
Our life events as not just segments
To pay into join on whim
But pleasure shared
With those still there
Is always new
And not indifferent
Let us stay to talk about it
Culture is that shared experience
And what we all crave

Astra and Sebastian

Come meet them all
Some regulars
Some only here when they don't know
I'm sure they'd love to hear your story
It'll help us all to share it through
And you both too
For more have travelled
On this road
That you'd imagine
Now go sit down
Until you leave
To live the future you inhabit
I'll get a drink
So we can toast the fresh new air
Some water for you both I think
It's really good to have you here

Astra and Sebastian

Illustrations
by Shelley Knowles-Dixon

The Ram's Tale	145
Astra emerging from the cave	146
Sebastian returns to find his home town burning	147
A Floating Island	148

Astra and Sebastian

Astra and Sebastian

Astra and Sebastian

Astra and Sebastian

The Ram's Tale
The Ram he led them seemed to grow
His bass voice deep a gentle bellow
To tell the truth I need to show you
Who I think that you should know

Astra emerging from the cave
Forever looked beyond the wood
To find the one who might engage
Her love reveal her power release
The knower and the known on stage

Sebastian returns to find his home town burning
Hot flame licked smoke fought with the rain
As all the fireflies in his brain
Danced off to die with falling truth

A Floating Island
She slept like the cast
Of a fairy tale woven
Together and into
Its own simple spell

Astra and Sebastian

Appendix
Brief Discussion of the Themes and Symbolism in *Astra and Sebastian*

"Astra and Sebastian" is an epic adventure in the tradition of an ancient hero myth, but brought up to date by having two heroes, both a man and a woman, thus presenting the story from both perspectives and also showing how perceived earthly opposites are reconciled by the universe.

"Astra and Sebastian" deals specifically with the change from child to adult but, as with any hero myth, this journey is applicable to any transitional moment in life. Hero myths throughout history articulate the symbolic journey of self discovery or individuation using archetypal motifs that we find in the unconscious. Cultures would build this psychological profile into their stories to aid the physical journey through life. Even today in a secular society, without help from any formal mythology, we undertake the journey of a hero unconsciously, every time we fall in love, face a crisis, or change, and any time we embark on a project.

For a detailed breakdown of the hero myth, a great place to start is *The Hero With A Thousand Faces* by Joseph Campbell.

The story of Astra and Sebastian also evokes the cycle of constellations through which the earth appears to move every day, year and precessional [*sic*] cycle; the two heroes encounter manifestations of each of these twelve constellations, from Aquarius to Capricorn, as they proceed with their journey. This celestial progression is the only universal measure of time and evocative of the cosmogonic [*sic*] cycle of creation, preservation, destruction and rebirth.

Astra and Sebastian's celestial journey is meant to emphasize the second important theme in the poem, that of cycles within cycles and the harmony between them. In the poem, "Astra and Sebastian", the last chapter represents Aquarius, this being the constellation marking the next precessional age we have just entered, which provides a sense of continuation rather than completion. By moving the setting

Astra and Sebastian

of the poem to the modern age the cycle continues but with a new flavour and we have the beginnings of a spiral which is more representative of nature than the circle. Music provides an example of this: a cycle or perfect fifths does not bring you back to the note you started with; there is a small discrepancy in the frequency known as the Pythagorean comma.

1. The Cave
Astra is representative of the spirit, the concept, the universe or infinity. Although still a child on earth she has seen many things.

2. Meanwhile In The Market
Sebastian represents the body, the object, the earth or the singular. The castle is representative of all earthly hierarchies and the need for physical endeavour in order to feed the physical form. Julia is Aquarius, the water bearer, and represents the need for something more than just physical, something that is often ignored in a place like the castle.

3. Home
This chapter discusses the roles and hierarchies that are often played out within the isolated independent homes of a competitive market economy which can often lead to the development of neurosis. It also shows how Sebastian is still a child.

4. A Day Of Knights
The knights represent material gain based upon war and Sebastian the elder's words to Sebastian, although wise, show that he is still in control of his son's future.

5. Which Witch Is Which
The Wise Old Woman is an archetypal figure and gives Sebastian the help he will need later in the story. This comes in the forms of knowledge, a lump of sweet wax and self confidence.

Astra and Sebastian

6. Keep The Home Fires Burning
The destruction of Sebastian's home town is symbolic of the end of childhood and the beginnings of personal responsibility. Astra knows Sebastian, and Sebastian thinks he has met Astra somewhere before. — This is because they are opposite physical manifestations of the universal whole. — She is the known, the entire universe and he is the knower, the built rational world. He feels compelled to rescue her, so he can become master of his own universe. And she can allow herself to be consumed by her opposite. Later in the poem the roles will be reversed and Sebastian will give himself up to Astra and she will become master of her own universe, that is, the stars.

7. Escape
The running away represents the teenage need for rebellion and self control but, as yet, without any direction. The forest represents that place of intrigue and wild physicality which is the entry to adulthood. The clearing is a place of introspection where the two can reflect upon their childhood but hopefully avoid getting trapped there forever. This is all manifested in the two fishes in the pool which are Pisces, the thoughtful end of the celestial year.

8. The Golden Ram
The Ram is Aries, the beginning of the celestial year offering the choice to begin the adventure, here, of adulthood and become a hero. The two potential heroes have to leave the clearing of their old known existence and accept the adventure ahead willingly, rather than being forced to do so. Otherwise, they will not be able to appreciate the potential wisdom it has to offer.

9. The Ram's Tale
The Ram and his friends are archetypal figures who exist in the unconscious but must be manifested by the conscious mind if they are to be of any help in understanding our own journey and its relationship to those who have gone before us. The quest for the life-affirming water of life — although a journey to discover

the self — is equally the concreting of these somewhat vague images into a certain knowledge of the true nature of the universe. This process — whereby metaphysical concepts are given as much physical weight and presence as material objects — can be termed Reification and allows an equality to be recognised between the conceptual and material, so we can avoid a wholly materialistic existence, which is generally unfulfilling, as representative of half only of the available universe and subject to the cosmogonic cycle which involves destruction, unlike the permanence to be found in an eternal concept.

10. The Chasm Challenge
The chasm represents the somewhat overwhelming physical world which can encourage one to retreat inside ones self, distracted by the menial and insignificant or by the promise of greater glory ahead.

11. Siren's Bell
The angels represent the first sexual callings of adolescence. The angels turn into crones when Sebastian remembers Astra because at that moment he accepted the feminine within and no longer needs gratification from without. This is the conquering of the childlike dependence upon the mother and offers the chance for developing lasting, loving and empowering relationships.

12. Astra's Journey
This is the alternate experience of sexual awakening. The prince must not be succumbed to or you will forever be living in subservience to the image of the father.

13. The Bull Ring
As well as overcoming the image of the parent of the opposite sex, each hero must defeat the dominating presence of the parent of the same sex if they are to be their own master and shape their own world. The bull is Taurus, symbol of earth.

14. On The Road
The road represents the certainty of choosing your own path through life. The fact that the two heroes are clinging to each other and speaking in unison means that they are overawed by this amazing new world drenched in the light of awakening and do not yet have the confidence to express themselves as individuals. The monster is the Trickster archetype and represents the physical world of creation through destruction. Sebastian and Astra conquer him and the superficial dichotomies of physical existence by staying true to what they know and remaining as a universal whole, refusing his attempts to separate them and thus the opposites that they represent. This discourse allows the coyote to discover his one true self — the playful Trickster beneath the surface — and be content with it; whilst at the same time Astra and Sebastian — through their success — begin to grow in confidence and to see themselves as individuals. We focus on them now as representing the two different aspects of Gemini, the cosmic twins.

15. Karkenios
The town represents growth for the sake of itself, without caring what gets destroyed or even what it achieves. This mode of thought puts you out of step with natural cycles, represented by the crab, and demands some form of compensation from you, some sacrifice. The whole chapter is about the interplay between two symbolic forms of cancer. — Karken means cancer in Greek, and the word carcinogenic is derived from this. Karkenios means city of the crab.

16. The Show
The young girl is the sacrifice needed for the king, his children and the city to be removed from the cosmogonic cycle and acquire personal gain or wealth. Sebastian and Astra are experimenting with their individuality and ideals but soon discover this requires personal responsibility which can lead to physical hardship.

Astra and Sebastian

17. The Crab
The crab is Cancer and represents the temple to which you must give yourself up, travel to the inner sanctum and free yourself of all earthly ego trappings, uniting yourself with the infinite universe, to emerge as an individual. Taking the heroes' example the king frees the town by finally taking responsibility for his actions and gives himself back to the cosmogonic cycle, allowing his children the freedom to grow and develop their world.

18. Drift
The sea is the freedom of the true individual to relax and free him or herself of their goals whilst at the same time trusting the universe to carry them over the edge of the day and towards their future needs. The kiss represents that Sebastian and Astra, as individual adults, finally understand their attraction for each other and choose to come together in mutual empowerment and with the knowledge of true love. The self awareness of all this, after the fact, is manifested by the storm.

19. Lion Trial
The lion is Leo and here represents the fear of wondering if you can live up to your true power as an individual. This fear can eat you up unless you validate your individuality by asking for help. As a true individual this won't feel like any admission of failure but an acceptance of growth.

20. An Elemental Temple
The voice is your inner voice, which you can hear and listen to once you have conquered fear and which will lead through light and dark, away from physical baggage to the centre of your true self. Astra and Sebastian have been into a temple before (the crab) so have no difficulty passing each gate or arriving in the lit inner sanctum of clarity (rather than the dark inner void of possession). The statues are the creator and the destroyer. Astra and Sebastian recognise their place in the middle, beyond the history on the walls, as preservers. So they finally manifest the

union of the one with the infinite, of the physical with the mystical, by making love.

21. Rising Up and Away
The scales are Libra, the equality of difference and the unification of from and to, which is manifested as the balance of opposites in every physical object. Finally, in the complementary act to that which occurred in, "Keep The Home Fires Burning", Astra is master of her own universe and Sebastian succumbs to his opposite. Having achieved this knowledge together they are the entirety of the universe manifested.

22. The Land Of Ne'er Destroyed
The temple is a ruin because the heroes have no more need for its symbolic power now that they understand their true nature and their position in relation to the greater cycle. The Land Of Ne'er Destroyed is the mountain of knowledge, the sum total of the lessons of history, economics and politics which are there for any brave soul, who has accepted the universe, to learn. The spider is Orion, in the form in which he is depicted by the Nazca Lines; although he is not in the cosmological cycle, he traditionally looks after the dead.

23. A Floating Island
The scorpion is Scorpio and represents the acquisition of knowledge. The lady is the mother goddess and at her navel, out of the essence of the universe, grows the world tree which is the axis of the earth. The axis of the earth is at an angle to the ecliptic, the plane of our orbit. As the earth rotates, our axis appears to wobble against the backdrop of the fixed stars. This movement means the pole star changes with the generations and also creates the 26000 year precessional cycle, or the movement of the rising sun at the vernal equinox through the constellations lying on the celestial equator. (From Aquarius to Pisces.) This knowledge of time is contained within many ancient creation myths.

Astra and Sebastian

24. A Magical Flight
The arrow is Sagittarius and represents the inevitable progress to the future and thus, the heroes' return to physical reality. The return of the water functions to confirm the completion of the heroes' task and the Ram's horn can now be replaced on its stub. Astra and Sebastian have discovered the true essence of the universe and don't need symbolic access to it anymore, in the same way as they didn't need the temple any more on the beach. The Ram broke his horn off in the first place only as a means of accompanying them on their journey and to provide eventually a physical marker for the end of this cycle of their epic journey.

25. The Return
The centaur is Sagittarius. The reluctance of Sebastian to leave the mountain and the Ram is a means to consider the greatest potential failing of a hero, the refusal of the return. This is the temptation of successful heroes not to share their rewards and to refuse the final challenge of a return to the physical world, with its accusations, demands and other sensory trauma, but instead to remain closeted inside their own mind keeping their wisdom for themselves.

26. A New Age
The tramp is Capricorn and knows of their journey so has no need to succumb to the standards of his age. They have been spending time inside themselves, the universe, where time moves much faster, so that, when they return to physical reality, hundreds of years, not one, have passed. Astra and Sebastian are now experiencing the final aspect to the hero journey, that of dealing with change and the responsibility of communicating the importance of their own journey to others under the influence of an often hostile or ignorant reality. Sebastian's mother is Aquarius and her reappearance at the end signifies that she cannot be killed (or made to disappear) by any machinations of humankind. She represents the eternal dawn of the new precessional age and the presence of a universal cycle which eternally exists beyond the length or fragility of all human life.

Astra and Sebastian

Early Responses to *Astra and Sebastian*

Illsley's *Astra and Sebastian* is a poetic saga that strives towards timeless spectacle, through a textual feast for the senses. This is imaginative, phantasmagoric verse on a grand scale; in which heroic myth, punctuated by motifs of the dream-work and the unconscious, draws the reader into the human quest for love, self-knowledge, adventure and transcendence.
— Mary-Jane Newton, author of the poetry collection, *Of Symbols Misused*

What a massive grand opera L.W Illsley has maestroed with éclat here. A mighty epic poem replete with myth, legend and myth-legend. A veritable concantenation of events and creatures and eventful creatures. A vital panorama of goodies and baddies grappling and battling. Archetypes, typecasts, symbols, synecdoches in a brave brew of brouhaha. A cornucopia of humour and wit flashing their lashings via Mr Rhyme and his cousin Half. Dive in and delight. Plunge in and plunder. There's more than enough here to whet your appetite and whip up your acumen. The tale Astra and Sebastian partake in is our own if I'm not mistaken. In their resilience is our consilience. Demi-dream deliverance on a platter: "creating a future through mythology" indeed!
– Vaughan Rapatahana, author of the poetry collection, *Home, Away, Elsewhere*.

Astra and Sebastian

FIND OUT MORE ABOUT OUR AUTHORS, BOOKS, EVENTS AND INTERNATIONAL PRIZES

Visit our website
http://www.proversepublishing.com

Visit our distributor's website
<www.chineseupress.com>

Follow us on Twitter
Follow news and conversation: <twitter.com/Proversebooks>
OR
Copy and paste the following to your browser window and follow the instructions: https://twitter.com/#!/ProverseBooks

"Like" us on www.facebook.com/ProversePress

Request our E-Newsletter
Send your request to info@proversepublishing.com.

Availability
Most titles are available in Hong Kong and world-wide
from our Hong Kong-based Distributor,
The Chinese University Press of Hong Kong,
The Chinese University of Hong Kong, Shatin, NT,
Hong Kong SAR, China. Web: chineseupress.com

All titles are available from Proverse Hong Kong
and the Proverse Hong Kong UK-based Distributor.

We have stock-holding retailers in Hong Kong,
Singapore (Select Books),
Canada (Elizabeth Campbell Books),
Principality of Andorra (Llibreria La Puça, La Llibreria).

Orders can be made from bookshops in the UK and elsewhere.

Ebooks
Most of our titles are available also as Ebooks.

Astra and Sebastian

FIND OUT MORE ABOUT OUR AUTHORS, BOOKS, EVENTS AND INTERNATIONAL PRIZES

Visit our website
http://www.proversepublishing.com

Visit our distributor's website
<www.chineseupress.com>

Follow us on Twitter
Follow news and conversation: <twitter.com/Proversebooks>
OR
Copy and paste the following to your browser window and follow the instructions: https://twitter.com/#!/ProverseBooks

"Like" us on www.facebook.com/ProversePress

Request our E-Newsletter
Send your request to info@proversepublishing.com.

Availability
Most titles are available in Hong Kong and world-wide
from our Hong Kong-based Distributor,
The Chinese University Press of Hong Kong,
The Chinese University of Hong Kong, Shatin, NT,
Hong Kong SAR, China. Web: chineseupress.com

All titles are available from Proverse Hong Kong
and the Proverse Hong Kong UK-based Distributor.

We have stock-holding retailers in Hong Kong,
Singapore (Select Books),
Canada (Elizabeth Campbell Books),
Principality of Andorra (Llibreria La Puça, La Llibreria).

Orders can be made from bookshops in the UK and elsewhere.

Ebooks
Most of our titles are available also as Ebooks.

www.ingramcontent.com/pod-product-compliance
Lightning Source LLC
Chambersburg PA
CBHW042307230426
43662CB00031B/61